THE 3 DAY ENTREPRENEUR

How to Build a 6 or 7 Figure
Business Working Less
Than 3 Days a Week

William U. Peña, MBA

Dedication

To Matthew, my son, who gave me the best reason to
work less, and set the right priorities in my life.

To my wife, Genie, who put up with me for the last decade,
and is willing to continue.

To my mentor, David Finkel, who gave me the faith
that I could, "Have my cake, and eat it too."

And to God, who has been, and will always be, my friend.

Contents

Acknowledgement

Someone once said, that "When you stand on the shoulders of giants, it is easier to see over the mountain top." This book is a testament to that saying, since it was only possible because of the "giants" I have had the pleasure to get to know and learn from through the years. First, I want to thank David Finkel, who has been the greatest influence in my life in the world of business. In a time when I had a lot of energy, enthusiasm, but very little direction, you helped set me straight, and showed me the true path of success in business and life. I also want to thank the other "giants" whose books line my bookshelf, and who have been my guides in the past decade. These include Brian Tracy, Neil Rackham, Dan Kennedy, Anthony Robbins, Ken Blanchard, John Maxwell, Bill Cates, Michael Masterson, Chet Holmes, and the rest that are too numerous to count.

To Tim Ferris who had the guts to boldly bring the idea of working less and making more to the public's eye. To Scott Shane that had the determination to do the research and show the true face of entrepreneurship. To James Hunter who gave us the greatest book on leadership I have ever read, "The Servant."

I want to also thank the creators of Elance.com and Fiverr that made finding a quality team such an easy and fun experience. To my book editor Adina of Flamingo Design, whose talented work helped turn my convoluted manuscript into an actual book. To Kristen James who patiently took my crazy thoughts and turned them into something people could understand. To Angie, who designed my book cover, and gave me the first glimpse of what this book would be.

To my clients throughout the years, that paid me to experiment on them, and prove that the principles in this book truly work. To the 3 Day Entrepreneurs who shared their stories in this book, and who are the proof that you can build a 6 or 7 figure business working less than 3 days a week.

Last, it is also said, that "behind a great man, there is a great woman." Now I don't claim to be great, but I do claim to have a great woman at my side. To Genie, the love of my life, who has been a rock in spite all of the "crazy" that comes from living with an entrepreneur. Thank you for believing in me, expecting the best from me, and forgiving me when I was not on my best behavior.

Foreword by David Finkel

"**Y**ou're dropping out of college? Are you crazy?" I can still remember my family's reaction when I told them that I was dropping out of college to start my first company. My sisters used some strong language, to put it mildly. They were scared for me; they were looking out for my best interests; they didn't want to see me get hurt.

But what can you do with a stubborn, know-it-all 21 year old? Not much. Yet life had real lessons to teach me. That first start up failed, and my family breathed easier when I finished up my degree. That was until I started my second company. They were quieter about it this time, but they still had their "opinions.". Despite my first failure and my family's misgivings, I knew I wanted to build something more meaningful than just a resume of jobs in corporate America.

So I struggled, I flailed, I studied, and I persevered until the day eight years later when I became an "overnight" success. At that point, I had built one of the most successful niche business coaching companies in the United States, with over 1,500 clients and valued between $10-16 million.

It was during this wild ride that I learned the flexibility of history. At first my family and close friends thought I was crazy; later I become lucky; and finally, the day arrived when I learned that they always knew I could do it.

I share this with you because you're at a critical cusp in your business life,. a time when you can choose to follow old patterns to get yesterday's

+/- 10 percent, or grab on to a wholly new way of thinking about your business and enjoy exponential growth.

In this inspirational and concrete book, Will has laid out for you a detailed plan to upgrade your approach to creating and growing a business. His approach is values driven and has as its goal to help you create more by doing less.

Too many business owners try to brute force their way to success with longer hours and longer work weeks. But growing your business based solely on you personally producing more just further traps you in the business. Plus, there is a point past which you cannot progress—there just won't be any more hours in the day, or days in the week.

So what's the way out? Build a business, not a job. Look for ways to leverage your time to create more value. Get clear on what matters most in your life and build your business to support those priorities. All of these are themes covered in this book. Pay close attention. Do the action assignments Will lays out. The impact on your business, your family, and the world around you will be so worthwhile.

I still remember three questions that one of my business mentors shared with me after I had built and sold my first company for a large payday. She looked at me and, realizing exactly what I needed to hear, shared these three questions:

1. What matters most?

2. For the sake of what?

3. How much is enough?

Over time these questions have stayed with me, reminding me to keep my eyes on what my or any business is really about: creating value in the world so that I can better serve and contribute.

One of the things I admire most about Will's book is how intentional he is in his methodology to build businesses and wealth. He gets that financial success is a means to an end, not an end unto itself. All the dollars in the world won't create a home, or nurture a family, or contribute to a community. But in the right hands—your hands I hope—the wealth you build will be a blessing on a multitude of lives. Enjoy this book and let it be a great tool to help you succeed faster.

David Finkel

Founder and CEO of Maui Mastermind®

America's Premier Business Coaching Company

www.MauiMastermind.com

Introduction

I had never seen feet that small before. His hands were also so tiny compared to mine. I also got a kick watching his hand curl around my finger when I touched his little palm. Then the nurse handed him to me, and I took a gulp as I carefully took him in my arms. He seemed so delicate and felt light as a feather.

As I looked at him, I felt a surge of conviction telling me it was time for me to change the way I did things. I saw his little face and decided that day that I would do everything in my power to help that little boy reach his fullest potential in life. I would do whatever it took to help him succeed, and give him the encouragement he needed so that he could accomplish anything in life he desired.

But I knew in order to do that; I needed to make the time to spend with him. I knew that I needed to make the time to be with him, to eat with him, to walk with him, and to cry with him. I knew the 60 hours or so a week I was working would not allow me to those things, I knew it was time to make a big change in my life.

Soon after that, one of my very first mentors, David Finkel, shared his convictions to me and a group of 200 other people at one of his seminars. He declared, "I am not going to work more than 3 days a week, because I want to spend time with my family, and I will be successful regardless." Sure enough, he was, and he still is.

I remembered his pledge, and I made the same pledge when my first son was born. It's been 9 years since I made that pledge, and I have only worked, at most, 2–3 days a week in the entire time. I have consistently earned 6 figures and I am on my way to earning 7. All driven by my sole purpose: to make time to spend with my son, and help him grow into the best man he can possibly become. I was determined, and miraculously, opportunities kept appearing, clients kept coming, money kept flowing, and I was able to consistently enjoy a 4–5 day weekend with my family.

How was it possible? In this book, I will share the mindset, principles, and lifestyle that I worked hard to create in order to make my business revolve around my family life and not the other way around. These strategies will allow you to use the same amount of time and effort you are using now, or less, and multiply your returns 4, 5, or even 10 times as much as you are getting now.

Lastly, I will introduce you to other men and women, which I had the privilege to meet on my journey, who are also working 3 days or less, and some even as little as 5 to 10 hours a month. These individuals are also successfully making 6–7 figure incomes, while spending loads of quality time with their family and loved ones.

My promise to you is that if you make the effort to put these principles and strategies into practice, you will be able to work a 3 day workweek or less while building a 6–7 figure income. Even if you only put a few tips in this book to practice, I guarantee that you will be working a lot less than you are now, and making a lot more money. You may even take it further and build great wealth for yourself and your family, all while having plenty of time to enjoy the journey.

Though I do promise it will be simple, I cannot promise that it will be easy or comfortable. Success never is. But if you are committed to expanding your comfort zone to learn a new way of thinking and a new way of living, then you are just a few decisions away from living the exciting lifestyle of the 3 Day Entrepreneur.

PART I

Introducing the
3 Day Entrepreneur

CHAPTER

1

The Great Entrepreneur Problem

"Whenever you find yourself on the side of the majority, it is time to pause and reflect."
Mark Twain

Did you know that the average business owner works approximately 10 hours a day? Not only that, but they also work an average of 6 days a week. And their one free day is generally spent worrying about the other 6 days.

Even more alarming, all of this hard work is not paying off for the average entrepreneur. Consider these statistics from the book, "The Illusions of Entrepreneurship," by Scott Shane:

- Approximately 67% of owner-operated businesses generate less than $10,000 in profits annually.

- The median typical profit of all owner-operated business is $39,000. (Federal Reserve Survey of Consumer Finances).

- The average self-employed person earns significantly less than the average person that works for somebody else.

- The typical entrepreneur earns less than the entry level salary of someone doing the same thing, but employed by somebody else.

What do these statistics tell you? It tells us that all the long hours and long days, long weeks, and big sacrifices we're making to build a small business are generating less income and satisfaction than if we were to work for someone else!

Now, I don't know about you, but when I first decided to become an entrepreneur, this was not what I had in mind. I looked forward to the freedom from having to work for someone else. I looked forward to the millions of dollars I would be pulling in. Also, I looked forward to retiring early and living the American Dream, both for myself and my family.

I am not the only one. Most entrepreneurs dream of the promise land of Entrepreneurship. Unfortunately, most only end up in a life of slavery to their schedules, clients, and the trap of self-employment. It's as if we become the victims of a cosmic bait and switch, where we are promised money and freedom, but instead we are duped of our life savings, our health, and our families, all while being left holding the bag with a really big hole in it.

The Great Entrepreneur Problem

Most people get into entrepreneurship in the hopes of finding freedom to direct their own lives, the freedom to get paid what they ask, and the freedom to build their own future. Sadly, while this is the biggest motivation for entrepreneurs, the opposite is what they actually receive.

This is a great mystery. Think about it for a minute. Isn't entrepreneurship supposed to provide the lifestyle that we've always wanted? Wasn't entrepreneurship supposed to rescue us from the rat race? And, wasn't entrepreneurship supposed to bring us the American dream?

The unfortunate truth is that the typical way people approach entrepreneurship actually robs them of their freedom. All of the dreams of freedom from an overbearing boss, or freedom from the stress of work, freedom to choose what you get paid, as well as freedom to create your future, are the reasons people get into entrepreneurship. Yet, instead of an overbearing boss, you end up with many overbearing bosses in the form of customers. Instead of reduced stress, you get more in the form of project deadlines, customer requests, filings for the IRS, etc. Instead of the freedom to choose what you get paid, you are desperately looking for the next customer that oftentimes is nowhere to be found.

In addition, the statistics clearly show that the average business owner is paid less than if they were working for someone else. Think about what this means. As an entrepreneur, you work twice as hard, have to endure more stress, and put your health and family at risk. While the person that is doing the same type of work for someone else is making just as much as you do (sometimes more), and all they have to do is show up. What makes it worse is that we think things will get better in the future. Yet, the only future that we end up with is full of the constant grind of being trapped by self-employment.

The Impact of the Entrepreneur Problem on Our Families

And what is the impact of the Entrepreneur Problem on our loved ones?

The best ones to ask are… You guessed it: our loved ones. However, that may not sit well with you because you know, as well as I do, that they probably have a mouthful to share with us.

You see, it is all too common that at some point the demands of family and business come into conflict in the life of the entrepreneur. It's a zero sum game. We don't have unlimited time, effort, resources or money, and as an entrepreneur, you eventually realize that either your family or your business will have to be sacrificed in order to feed the other. Unfortunately, for most entrepreneurs, it is usually the family.

What is most puzzling is the fact that most entrepreneurs generally say that spending more time with family is the main reason they became entrepreneurs in the first place. However, the current entrepreneur lifestyle does not allow this dream to be realized because it demands so much time and effort just to compete in the marketplace.

Even successful entrepreneurs have more customers to please and more plates to keep spinning to keep everything afloat. In addition, with more demands generally comes more spending. The entrepreneur will justify working more to pay the bills, and to meet the demands of the business. This eventually keeps the vicious cycle going endlessly until the family members become fed up with the situation, the entrepreneur burns out, or both.

Many a spouse has celebrated the day when a business owner went bankrupt, which meant they could have their husband or wife back. Broken yes, but back nonetheless.

How to Build a Successful Business Working Only 3 Days a Week

But does this have to be the destiny of every entrepreneur? Are all entrepreneur's doomed to the same bleak future? Is it possible to make more money, and have more precious time to spend with your family? In other words, is it possible to, "have your cake and eat it too?"

The answer is: Absolutely!

In fact, this is what separates those who do succeed and enjoy entrepreneurship from those that don't. These are the few entrepreneurs that consistently prove the statistics wrong. They are the entrepreneurs that earn 6, 7 or even 8 figures and don't work more than 2–3 days a week. They are the entrepreneurs that have great family lives because they have the time to devote to building a healthy family. They are the ones that enjoy a healthy lifestyle because they have the time and money to devote to their health. They are the ones that can sleep at night, because they know that their business is taken care of, even when they are not there.

And the word "stress," is a four letter word to them.

This book is about these types of people. We call them The 3 Day Entrepreneurs.

This book not only describes these people, but it gives you the principles they follow so that you can apply them to your own life. It will take you from living in the trap of self-employment, to building a thriving 6, 7 even 8 figure business that revolves around the life you want.

One thing you will also find out about these 3 Day Entrepreneurs is that they are not rocket scientists. In fact, some of these people are average entrepreneurs that want to succeed like all of us. However, what they do have is a set of overpowering values that motivate them to create the life they want and build their business around it.

You will realize from hearing their stories that their driving force is nothing less than an overwhelming desire to live the life that they want, on their terms, whether that is more money, more freedom, more time with family, or more fun in their life.

Now, I want to turn the attention to you. What kind of impact will living a 3 Day Entrepreneur lifestyle have in your life?

Exercise

Take out a sheet of paper and answer the following questions:

- What would you do with all the extra time you would have on your hands, if you could get all the work in your business completed in only 2–3 days a week?

- What would you do with all the extra money you would have, if you could make a 6 or 7 figure income?

- What would it mean to you, if you could spend less time working on your business, and more time with your family, or doing other things you love to do?

Like the examples in this book, if you live The 3 Day Entrepreneur lifestyle, you will experience these results. You will be able to join the ranks of thousands of entrepreneurs in America that have put away the 50–60 hour work weeks. These entrepreneurs have not only overcome the Entrepreneur Problem, they are now living a revolutionized life for the sake of their health, their families, and their dreams.

CHAPTER 2

Who is the 3 Day Entrepreneur?

"Entrepreneurs are simply those who understand that there is little difference between obstacle and opportunity and are able to turn both to their advantage."

Niccolo Machiavelli (The Prince)

Wes Lucus

Wes Lucus faced many challenges but created a profitable business and an enjoyable life for himself and family. He is the CEO and Founder of Gemini Technical Consulting Group, and his company helps businesses use technology as an accelerator for growth. They also work as a mobile IT department for small business, providing technical support, equipment sales, IT management and business consulting services.

Wes' Story

"I am a 3 Day Entrepreneur. I only work at most between 20-25 hours a week, and make 6 figures in my business, working my way to 7 figures. I decided to pursue the 3 Day Entrepreneur Lifestyle for one big reason: I saw what my father had to endure as I grew up, and I realized I wanted to do things differently with my family.

In my house growing up, my dad would take work wherever he could, which sometimes meant we would only see him on weekends. And because of the physical labor that he did, his body suffered—he's had several back surgeries, and both knees replaced. Seeing how much he sacrificed in order to provide for our family, I've been determined to find ways to provide for my own family without having to make those same sacrifices, and to show other business owners how to do the same.

When I think about what helped me to transition to the 3 Day Entrepreneur Lifestyle most, I would say automation is the key. I spent a lot of time early on in this business finding or designing ways for the computers to do as much work as they can. Automation has been the biggest thing to allow me to provide a lot of value without sacrificing time. For the things I couldn't automate, I focused on detailed documentation so I could add people to my team, and they could take care of those tasks. Now, my vision for my business is to have the whole business running without me. I'll be working on innovation—new ways to automate and new solutions to serve our customers, all while vacationing around Europe.

My advice for entrepreneurs that want to leverage themselves better is to take vacations. That's when you get to test your systems and see how well they run without you. When you get back, you might have a mess to clean up, but that's OK—now you know how to improve your systems so your next vacation will be better."

This is just one entrepreneur, out of others you will read about in this book, which have discarded the typical entrepreneur lifestyle for something better. Something, that serves them and their families in a much greater way.

Life First, Business Second

The 3 Day Entrepreneur is a person that has set their lives up to prioritize the things that are most meaningful to them. They put the things they hold most dear first, and then they do everything in their power to make their business or career fit this lifestyle. Most people put off their ideal lifestyle until they can make enough money to retire at a ripe old age, when it's almost too late to enjoy it. The 3 Day Entrepreneur, on the other hand, thinks lifestyle first, and then finds a way of building a successful 6 or 7 figure business around it.

The 3 Day Entrepreneur understands that happiness now has much more value than happiness later. So he or she designs the life they want for themselves to enjoy right now, and then creatively fit their business to support this lifestyle.

What motivates this special breed of entrepreneurs? The lifestyle that the 3 Day Entrepreneur creates means more time for family, more time for rest, more time to grow their wealth, or more time for more enjoyment of their life. The desire to live this lifestyle is so important to them, it becomes the driving force to do whatever it takes to create it and maintain it. Generally, this gives them the courage and strength to break through the many excuses and social norms of people who try to tell them that this kind of life is not possible.

The 3 Day Entrepreneurs are those special individuals that turn people's heads at parties. When asked what they do, people are amazed when they say they only work 2–3 days a week and make 6 or 7 figures. They are the dedicated homeschoolers, the month-long vacation travelers, the ever-present fathers and the community active mothers. They are the financially independent church pastors, the serial entrepreneurs, and the daytime investors. And let's not forget the independently wealthy surfers that spend most of their days at the beach.

They are the ones that have found the secret formula. They are not only able to reap the benefits of living the life they want presently, but are able to build a great life and financial foundation for their future as well.

The Value of Time

These entrepreneurs fully understand the value that time has in their lives. They see their time as a valuable commodity (even more valuable than money), and they spend it only on the things they consider to be of greatest importance to them: which is their family, their health, and profitable opportunities. Therefore, the big focus for the 3 Day Entrepreneur is to work the least amount of days possible, while creating as much money and wealth as possible.

It is not uncommon for the 3 Day Entrepreneur to enjoy a 5-day weekend. Generally, though, their schedule commonly consists of working no more than 3 days a week, or less than 30 hours over a few days in their week.

Creating Value in Less Time

As you read their stories, and read some of the strategies in this book, you will notice that the 3 Day Entrepreneur has many creative ways of creating more value in much less time and effort than the typical entrepreneur does. The 3 Day Entrepreneur can do this because they follow a special set of principles, live a very focused lifestyle, and use unique tools to create this way of life. They are able to leverage this 3 Day Lifestyle so effectively that they set themselves up to eventually be financially free. They are able create a situation where they are free to work when and how much they want, while still producing a substantial and even massive income.

This book is dedicated to revealing the principles and practices of those who currently live the 3 Day Lifestyle, so that you can take your current situation, and turn it into the kind of lifestyle that will benefit you, your family and your future.

PART II

The 3 Day Entrepreneur Mindset

The power behind the 3 Day Entrepreneur comes from a unique way of thinking and by devoting oneself to living by 4 core commitments. These commitments lead the 3 Day Entrepreneur to making the best choices, resulting in the greatest return for their time, effort resources and money.

The 4 Core Commitments of the 3 Day Entrepreneur are:

- The Commitment to Create Massive Value.
- The Commitment to Leverage Time, Effort, Resources and Money (TERM).
- The Commitment to Automate Everything.
- The Commitment to Never Ending Improvement.

Before one can live the 3 Day Entrepreneur Lifestyle, you need to master the 3 Day Entrepreneur mindset. Many have tried to create a lifestyle where they work less, and make more money. But, they find themselves stressed and unable to enjoy their freedom, or not able to make enough money to sustain their lifestyle.

This reminds me of a friend who lost 50 pounds, but put it back on a few months later. When I asked him what happened, he said, "Even though I was skinny on the outside, I was still fat on the inside."

The 3 Day Entrepreneur spends time mastering these 4 Core Commitments. Once these commitments begin to influence all their choices, then they will start reaping the benefits and rewards that come from the 3 Day Entrepreneur Lifestyle.

But before we dig into the mindset of the 3 Day Entrepreneur, I want to introduce you to another special person:

Louis Lautman

Louis Lautman is an entrepreneur and success coach who has contributed greatly to young entrepreneurs by creating a virtual society of other young like-minded, motivated business people, called the Young Entrepreneur Society. Louis also wanted to create a platform for young people who were looking for more in their lives and so he produced The YES Movie, an enlivening documentary that has become a catalyst for inspiring passion in young entrepreneurs everywhere, in business and life. Louis is also the CEO and Founder of Supreme Outsourcing, a virtual assistant and outsourcing company.

Louis is a very special individual. I say Louis is special because not only does he make over 6 figures, he has also been able to convert 90% of his work into fun, so the work he does is no longer work at all. This earns him a place in the 3 Day Entrepreneur club, since he is able to pick the life he wants, and then design a business around it. This is what Louis says about the 3 Day Entrepreneur lifestyle:

Louis' Story

"My definition of Lifestyle Mastery is when the people who know you best don't know the difference between your work and your play. So most people would not know if I am working or not. For me it is effortless, and I only engage in pleasurable activities. So you could say 2-3 hours a week or you could say 40-50, but lunches, dinner and drinks with friends is not that difficult.

And when people ask me what my main motivation is, I tell them it is to make as much money as possible while only doing work I enjoy.

If I were to give advice to any entrepreneurs out there that want to live the 3 Day Entrepreneur lifestyle, it would be to sell something with a high ticket price, where you can make recurring revenue, and make sure it has as few moving parts as possible that you don't need to manage."

CHAPTER 3

The Foundation of the 3 Day Entrepreneur Mindset

"An army of principles can penetrate where an army of soldiers cannot."
Thomas Paine

There are some natural laws that work in favor of the person that dedicates themselves to becoming a 3 Day Entrepreneur. These laws are universal, meaning it applies to many people no matter what country, gender, culture, and background you are from. It seems that sometime during Creation, our Creator wired us with these resources right in our DNA.

These natural principles are what make it possible for any entrepreneur to become a 3 Day Entrepreneur. Therefore, if any entrepreneur can learn to align themselves with these principles, they can begin to create massive value that will result in more and more money and freedom.

The Pareto Principle
(Also known as the 80/20 Rule)

The Pareto Principle is named after Italian economist Vilfredo Pareto. Pareto observed in 1906 that 80% of the land in Italy was owned by 20% of the population, and he further observed this principle in many other aspects of the natural world.

The principle comes from how different groups, whether people or products, tend to create a situation where 20% of the group eventually produces 80% of the results, while 80% of the group produces 20% of the results.

The greatest impact of the 80/20 rule is found in the fact that it applies to almost every group. It applies to groups of people, products, animals, and even flowers. Though the exact quantity does not matter--it could be 70/30, 95/5, even 60/40--the natural tendency is for a small portion of the group to produce the greatest impact in the group.

This makes the 3 Day Entrepreneur's lifestyle possible for anyone determined enough to focus their time and efforts to finding and doing only the 20% of tasks that bring 80% of the results—and delegating, automating, or deleting all the parts that bring the least value. Any person that dedicates themselves to doing only the most valuable tasks in a business will eventually find themselves making a lot more money, and creating more and more time to enjoy it.

Parkinson's Law

The principle of Parkinson's Law was first described by Cyril Northcote Parkinson, and says that, "Work expands so as to fill the time available for its completion." In other words, the amount of time you set aside to perform a task eventually becomes the amount of time that it takes you to complete that task.

We've all had the experience when we believe we only have a small amount of time to complete a project, and then it takes us exactly that long to finish it. For example, do you remember when you had a term paper due in high school or college? Often, I procrastinated and saved the paper until the last minute. Have you done that? And because you had only one day left for turning in the term paper, you would miraculously get it done in that one day—even though the teacher gave you 2 weeks to finish it. What this shows us is that it only takes 1 day to complete the term paper, but we spend the entire 2 weeks wasting time and effort stressing about it.

A common experience for many entrepreneurs is to spend an entire day working, but then feeling like they didn't get very much done. The cause? We don't put time limits on ourselves. If we don't put time limits on completing a task, we will naturally default to taking more time than was needed. Like water that settles to fill whatever space you put it in, so do our work habits according to Parkinson's Law. This ultimately results in the typical entrepreneur working twice, or even three times as hard, while producing minimal results.

The 3 Day Entrepreneur takes advantage of Parkinson's Law, because the opposite is also true. If we put smaller time limits on the work that we need to accomplish, we will find that we could finish all of our work within that small time. Even better, this forces us to focus on only doing the most valuable and more important tasks, and helps us to delegate or eliminate the work that is not as valuable.

Ockham's Razor

Ockham's Razor is a principle that came from a 14th century logician and Franciscan friar named William of Ockham. When applied to business the principle simply says, "The simplest solution is usually the best solution."

Now, you would assume that this is common sense. But some entrepreneurs have a tendency to complicate simple things, resulting in a massive waste of time, effort, resources and money. The 3 Day Entrepreneur, on the other hand, understands that if the simplest solution is the best solution, then there is always an opportunity to get the result you want by finding simpler and less costly ways of doing it. The 3 Day Entrepreneur dedicates themselves to using the "razor" to constantly shave off unnecessary time, effort, resources and money, while getting the same or a better result. The result is that it helps produce a greater return on investment because more is being created with less effort to create it.

Another name for this idea is called leverage.

Kaizen

Kaizen, Japanese for "improvement," refers to the philosophy that focuses on continuously improving the systems in any business.

Simply, the principle of Kaizen describes two main ideas: 1) There is always room for improvement, and 2) human beings have a natural tendency to waste time, effort, resources and money.

We would all agree that, as people, we are far from having reached our fullest potential. In a business full of groups of people, you see this in a greater way. With so many people, it creates a situation with a lot of room for improvement. Kaizen suggests that, even if you are getting good results for your current efforts, the opportunity exists for improvement, and then focusing time and effort to improving will greatly multiply your results. In other words, small improvements will result in exponentially greater results.

Human beings also have a tendency to waste valuable resources. This means that we have a tendency to put in a certain level of input, but not receive an equal level of output. Somewhere along the line, we create waste that results in us producing much less than we could. This is why most entrepreneurs experience working twice as hard, but taking home less and less money.

The 3 Day Entrepreneur makes it a priority to invest the time and effort toward continual improvement, knowing that small improvements in the organization will result in a greater and greater return on their investment. Making it a focus to reduce waste in different levels of an organization also tends to result in greatly boosting the bottom line.

Conclusion

These few but powerful principles that exist in nature create the opportunity for any dedicated person to live the 3 Day Entrepreneur Lifestyle. Focusing one's efforts on the 20% that brings 80% of results, limiting the amount of time spent accomplishing tasks, shaving off unnecessary work in search of simpler solutions, and investing time in continual improvement will produce massive results in terms of revenue, profits, and freedom. For the dedicated person, this makes the 3 Day Entrepreneur Lifestyle not only possible, but ultimately, inevitable.

CHAPTER 4

Commitment 1: Creating Massive Value

"Try not to become a man (or woman) of success, but rather try to become a man (or woman) of value."
Albert Einstein

- How many hours does Oprah Winfrey have in her day?
- How many hours does Donald Trump have in his day?
- How many hours do Warren Buffet, Bill Gates, Richard Branson, Jeff Bezos, and many other uber successful people have in their day?
- And how many hours do you and I have in our day?

I just have one last question for you: Why do these billionaires get the results that they do, and you get the results you do, when we all have the same amount of time in our day?

Do they have special powers? Are they aliens? Do they have special mutant genes that give them superhuman influence over the universe and the outcome of their lives? No? Then why do they get different results within the same 24 hours that you and I have?

The answer is simple. In those 24 hours, the things they do are very different from the things we do. It is not the amount of time a successful person uses that makes them successful, but rather what they do within that time. The things that successful people do in every hour produce a substantially higher return on investment than what other people normally do.

If we want to continue getting the results we are getting, then we just need to continue doing what we are doing. However, if we want greater returns for our efforts, like successful people do, then we need to do the things that bring a higher return on investment for every hour that we work.

In order to see this a bit more clearly, I want you to do a quick exercise:

Exercise

1. Take out a sheet of paper and write down everything that you did in your day yesterday. Now I want you to consider each of these tasks as investments that you made of your time "currency." Like a smart investor, you want to find out how much return you got for your investment, right?

2. Now write next to each task, the return on investment that you received, or that you can expect to receive for each task.

3. Now look at your list. How much return on investment did you get for all your hard work yesterday?

If you continue having days like yesterday, will the return on your investment of time and effort make you wealthier, and add more zeroes to your bank account? Or, were the things you did yesterday just wasted time and effort with no expectation for a profitable return?

What are the chances that if you continue doing the things you did yesterday, every day, that you will achieve your goal of building a 6, 7 or even 8 figure income?

Revealing isn't it?

When we look at what we spend our time and efforts on, you begin to realize why we are not billionaires, or even millionaires for that matter.

Therefore, the most important question we need to ask ourselves is, "If I were to change the tasks I do daily, and instead do the tasks that bring a greater return on investment; what kind of results will I produce? What kind of lifestyle will I create?"

This is the 3 Day Entrepreneur Mindset.

It's All about ROI

The 3 Day Entrepreneur Mindset is based on the idea that not all tasks are created equal. There are tasks that have a substantial greater return on investment than others. There are thousands of different ways of getting things done, so we can choose to do the things that bring the greatest value. Not only so, but we can also choose to do them using the least amount of our time, effort, resources and money.

Therefore, the 3 Day Entrepreneur focuses only on the highest value tasks in the organization, the tasks with the highest ROI. This results in an ever-increasing amount of value created, with much less time and effort doing it. In other words, it will result in a massive ROI yielding much more money, while requiring less time to produce it.

The Power of "Only"

In order to consistently create a massive ROI, the 3 Day Entrepreneur lives by one very simple and powerful word. And that word is "Only."

The word "Only" defines the tasks they choose to do, and therefore it determines their future success.

The 3 Day Entrepreneur will focus all of their attention on the tasks that bring the highest return on investment, doing ONLY these things and nothing more.

How does the 3 Day Entrepreneur get everything else done? They use every tool in this book to off-load anything in their organization that does not create massive value for them or their business.

What is Value?

The biggest focus for the 3 Day Entrepreneur is to create the most value possible. But what is value? The 3 Day Entrepreneur defines value as something that is in such great demand in the marketplace that people would be willing to trade massive amounts of money or other resources in order to get it.

Therefore, as a 3 Day Entrepreneur, our attitude is that if we cannot trade it in the marketplace, we don't do it. In other words:

"If it doesn't make money, someone else can do it."

The 3 Day Entrepreneur is therefore always looking for ways to transform whatever they do into an opportunity to make money, so that they can get a greater ROI for their efforts.

From Will

 The other day I had a dinner meeting with some friends, and the evening could have ended in us just having a fun, entertaining and pleasant time with very little return. Instead, I decided to bring up some topics that led everyone at that meeting to brainstorm together, so that we could generate a greater ROI from our dinner meeting. Great ideas were exchanged that a few months later led to 5–6 figure results for a few of us.

The Value Creation Question

In order to constantly create value, the 3 Day Entrepreneur uses a set of guidelines and principles to keep focused on what is valuable. These guidelines prevent them from being distracted by the thousands of low value items that are constantly clamoring for their attention.

Without guidelines, we would fall back into the same problems that plague the typical entrepreneur. This is why the 3 Day Entrepreneur does not just use these principles as nice affirmations to think about during the day. Rather, they govern every decision. In essence, their businesses live and die by these guidelines.

The 3 Day Entrepreneur's principles are in the form of value-creation questions that they repeatedly ask themselves every day.

1. What is the most valuable thing I could be doing right now (or, in this situation; or today)?

2. How can I multiply the value of what I am currently doing even more?

3. (When facing an obstacle) What valuable opportunities has this situation opened up for me?

4. How can I do things differently to create an even greater ROI with what I am doing?

5. (And my favorite…) How can I do all this in a way that is fun for me and makes me a lot of money?

Conclusion

The 3 Day Entrepreneur is driven by their desire to create massive value in every situation, and they determine that value by how much money their actions bring them. They are determined to identify the tasks that bring the highest value, and to ONLY do these tasks. This leads them to constantly ask themselves the Value Question, so that every hour of their day results in a massive return on their investment of time, effort, resource and money.

The 3 Day Entrepreneur also understands that value can be maximized through the use of leverage. In other words, as they create value, they can continue to find ways to reduce the amount of time, effort, resources, and money they use, further increasing their ROI. This is the topic of our next chapter...

CHAPTER
5

Commitment 2:
Leveraging Time, Effort,
Resources, and Money

> "Progress isn't made by early risers.
> It's made by lazy men trying to find
> easier ways to do something."
> **Robert A. Heinlein**

Leverage is a Four Letter Word (TERM)

What is leverage?

According to the dictionary, leverage is "the ability to influence a system, or an environment, in a way that multiplies the outcome of one's efforts—without a corresponding increase in the consumption of resources." In other words, leverage is using the least amount of time, effort, resources and money, (also known as TERM) in order to produce a more valuable return.

For example, imagine you have 5 potential sales prospects that you need to meet. You can meet one potential prospect at a time, spending an hour of your time at each appointment. This of course uses your gas and time driving to the appointment locations, uses your paper to deliver your proposal, and more, all in the hopes that you will land each one of the five prospects and turn them into a client. If your sales ratio is say 60%, you may land 3 out of the 5 prospects as a client.

On the other hand, you can have 20 potential prospects come and meet you at the conference room in your executive suite or office. Then you spend an hour of your time giving them a powerful sales presentation. You sell 60% of the room and end up with 12 clients.

By using a different method of approaching the same situation, you were able to use less of your:

- **Time**—You used 1 hour instead of 5.

- **Effort**—All you had to do was put together 1 presentation rather than 5.

- **Resources**—You saved gas because you didn't drive anywhere, and saved paper by sending digital copies of the presentation to everyone.

- **Money**—You spent nothing extra because the conference room is included in your monthly office rent.

So, you spent a quarter of your resources and landed twice the amount of clients.

This is the essence of leverage.

In the previous chapter we spoke of identifying and doing the tasks that bring the highest return on investment. As you do these high value tasks, you can increase your return on investment further by using less time, effort, resources and money to accomplish them.

The Leverage Question

Just as there are Value Creation Questions that help you produce more value, there are also Leverage Questions that help you use more leverage. This is what I call the "Instead Of..." principle of leverage. Here are a few examples:

Instead of spending 10–20 hours a week marketing, why not convince an experienced marketing company to do all of the marketing for you for free. You can pay them by referring them 4–5 new customers in exchange for free marketing services.

Instead of going out and using your time, effort, resources and money doing your own sales appointments, why not contract a commissioned sales person to get leads, set appointments, and convert those leads for you?

Instead of coming up with new profitable business ideas on your own, why not gather a group of great creative minds together and have them come up with the ideas for you? You can give them a share of the future profits or an ownership stake in your new venture.

Here are a few more "Instead Of" questions that the 3 Day Entrepreneur asks, which leads to creating more value, while using better leverage:

- Instead of doing things this way, how can I do it in a way that creates more value, while using less time, effort, resources or money (a.k.a.: TERM)?

- Instead of doing this myself, who can I delegate it to someone who will get the best results for this?

- Instead of spending any of my time, effort, resources and money on this, how can we get it done using someone else's TERM?

The list goes on and on...

By asking the "Instead Of" question, our mind begins to creatively come up with many different and new ideas to approach a situation with vastly greater leverage. As a matter of fact, just taking the time to consider a more leveraged way of doing things will put us leagues ahead of what entrepreneurs typically do.

Here is a good exercise to demonstrate this for you.

Exercise

1. Take out a sheet of paper and list some tasks that commonly take up a lot of your time, effort, resources and money.

2. Now for every task, ask yourself the "Instead Of" question:

   "Instead of doing things this way, what is a better way to do this using less time, effort, resources and money?"

3. Give your mind time to process this, and begin writing some different more leveraged ways to approach this task. Or go to some of your advisers, partners, and employees and ask them the same question (use leverage to get the leverage question answered…).

What you will begin to see is that there are many different and better ways of doing things. Some of those ways can even give us 2, 3, or even 10X greater return, while using less and less of our time and effort. Can you now begin to see why the 3 Day Entrepreneur Lifestyle is not only doable, but also highly profitable?

Conclusion

The 3 Day Entrepreneur mindset is governed by the principle that there is a much better, easier, quicker, more leveraged way of doing things. And they run their businesses by constantly seeking answers to the leverage question, in everything that they do.

So "instead of" working 5–6 days a week trying to build your business, how can you get it all done in 2 or 3 days a week?

CHAPTER 6

Commitment 3: Automating Everything

"The purpose of automation is to free us from the tyranny of doing unnecessary work."

Will Peña

The third part of the 3 Day Entrepreneur mindset is the ability to automate as much as we can, in order to free us up to focus on other, more valuable efforts.

If you can create value, and you can create leverage, then it will multiply your returns even greater when you can create a system that can do it all for you. Since the system is not dependent on you, it frees you up to create even more value elsewhere.

What is Automation?

For The 3 Day Entrepreneur, the definition of automation is simply being able to get the highest quality result without it being dependent on one person (especially you).

Now, you may be thinking, like many entrepreneurs do, that this is not possible because, "If you need something done well, you have to do it yourself!"

Well, the only question I have for you is, "When was the last time you saw the CEO of Wal-Mart ringing up the next customer?"

The truth is that successful corporations are effectively run via automating all of the processes in the organization through delegation, systemization, and outsourcing. In fact, I would even dare to say that you are not a true business owner unless you are looking for more and more ways to automate. If your business revolves around you then you do not have a business, you have self-employment, which in today's economy is one-step above (and sometimes below) working a job.

The 3 Day Entrepreneur, on the other hand, is constantly looking for more and more ways to automate, and free him or herself of the day-to-day operations of the business. If he or she can create a business that runs itself, then it is no longer a business, but a profitable asset that they can later sell for top dollar.

The 3 Day Entrepreneur holds to the very powerful success principle that says:

"A person's success is proportional to the amount of things they let go of."

The Benefits of Automation

There are many benefits to automation, more than we can cover in this one chapter. But we will discuss the most impactful benefits that fuel the 3 Day Entrepreneur Lifestyle. These include:

1. **Freeing up your time**—For every percentage of work you automate, you are freeing a greater percentage of time for yourself. You can either take back that time (hence the 3 day workweek) or you can invest that time in creating even more value for the business.

2. **Freeing up your efforts**—If it is no longer up to you to make the operation work, but it continues to generate satisfied customers, efficient workflow, and happy employees, then you can focus more of your efforts on other high value tasks in the business.

3. **Freeing up your resources**—Let's face it. You and your people are the greatest resource of your company. If you can free yourself and your leaders up, then you will be able to focus on other areas of the business that will result in greater revenue and profit.

4. **Freeing up your money**—Remember that time means money. Being the top dog in the company makes you the highest paid person (or supposedly highest paid person) in the business. By freeing yourself up, you are no longer wasting that valuable time and money doing things in your business that bring little value.

The Automation Question

The 3 Day Entrepreneur understands that automation is a mindset. And just like value and leverage, it comes from the 3 Day Entrepreneur asking themselves the automation question:

> **"How can I get this done in a way that creates great value, but is not dependent on me (or any one person)?"**

By asking this question, it puts you in the frame of mind to begin coming up with ideas on how to automate your tasks, and improve them in the process.

Now, the 3 Day Entrepreneur doesn't just think about automation once in a while, we think about it constantly. Even in the most mundane and simple tasks, the 3 Day Entrepreneur is looking for ways to automate.

Automation Through Elimination

One of the best ways to automate is by eliminating unnecessary steps from your usual routine. Less steps automatically means less use of your time and effort, or less use of someone else's.

What we don't realize is that there is always a more streamlined way to do something if we would just take the time to improve it. The 3 Day Entrepreneur does this by asking the Elimination question:

"Instead of doing this in multiple steps, how can I get it all done in just one step (or less steps)?"

What you will find is that by taking the time to find ways to get the system done in less steps, you not only shave off a lot of unnecessary work, but you sometimes get a higher quality result in the process.

Exercise

1. Pick a task, project, or routine that you do consistently.

2. List out all of the steps involved.

3. Brainstorm a way of eliminating a few steps from the task, by either deleting it, delegating it or designing a way to get it done without you.

4. Try your new routine without these tasks.

5. Every few weeks continue to find more ways to eliminate steps in your task, project, or routine, but still produce a high quality result.

High Quality Automation

Now, effective automation has to continue to produce a high quality product or service. It is not enough just to pass the buck, if the buck or responsibility is not fulfilled adequately either by a human, system, or machine. Therefore, a very important aspect of The 3 Day Entrepreneur automation mindset is that, "Effective automation always results in high quality results."

In others words:

- If you delegate, delegate to someone that will get optimal results.

- If you systematize, make sure the system delivers an optimal result.

- If you use technology, make sure the output is the best output it could spit out.

- If you outsource, make sure the outsource team delivers high quality work.

Conclusion

The 3 Day Entrepreneur is constantly searching for ways to automate everything, both large and small. The way he or she does this is by constantly asking the Automation Question. All with the understanding that effective automation is only achieved when they can continue to create a high quality product or service, and do it in a way that is not dependent on just one person.

CHAPTER 7

Commitment 4: Never Ending Improvement

"However beautiful the strategy, you should occasionally look at the results."
Winston Churchill

Up to this point we've seen that the 3 Day Entrepreneur Mindset means 3 things:

1. Creating value by focusing on the highest value tasks in an organization.

2. Using the least amount of time, effort, resources, and money to accomplish them.

3. Automating everything so that the results are not dependent on any one person.

And by doing all of these, you will begin to create a higher return on investment for every hour you spend in your business.

Now, doing these 3 things will be able to shave off 2–3 days from your week, and will bring you substantially greater returns in revenue, profit, equity, and more. However, if you want to continually grow in your impact, you need to continually review and improve on your efforts. This is the fourth powerful aspect of the 3 Day Entrepreneur mindset: the search for continual improvement.

The essence of continual improvement is that it is not enough to make something work—we must continually improve on it. In other words:

"If it's not broken, improve on it."

Why, you ask, should we improve on something that is working just fine for us? Here are a few reasons:

1. **Since there are multitudes of ways of accomplishing something, statistically there is probably a better way of doing what you are currently doing.**

   There is always another way to create more value, while using the least amount of time, effort, resources and money. Imagine you're working 5–6 days a week and getting a certain level of return for your efforts. It's not ideal, but you can tolerate it. Then, you put to practice some of the practical advice from this book, and you shave 2 or 3 days off your schedule. So you're able to accomplish the same amount of results in less time.

   You could stop there, since this is a great place to be. You have more freedom, more time to do the things you would like to do, and you are making the same amount of money.

   However, what if there was a way you could work 3 days a week and make twice as much money? Wouldn't you like to know about it? What if you could work 3 days a week and instead of a 6 figure salary, you can make a 7 figure salary? Wouldn't you like to know how to do it?

Or what if there was a way you could work 10 hours a month and generate a 7 figure income? Would that be something you would be interested in?

You get my point here. Why settle for just getting a little better than you were yesterday? Why not continue to grow so that you can reap greater and greater rewards from your efforts, and benefit yourself and your family?

The 3 Day Entrepreneur mindset allows you to pick the lifestyle you want, build a business around it, and if you choose, later you can improve on it.

2. **The market is ever changing, and your competitors are in a race to get your customers.**

In today's changing marketplace, there is a law among consumers called the "Law of Diminishing Returns." Yesterday's value becomes today's expectation. And what is expected is usually not very valuable.

We have to provide ever-increasing value in the marketplace to retain our current clients, or someone more handsome, charming, or beautiful, with bigger promises and shinier toys will come along and steal the hearts of our customers away from us.

Believe me when I tell you, that your competitors are jealously eyeing your customers and are plotting to woo them away from you as you read this. Why? Because a tighter economy means less customers. In addition, with fewer customers, the only other place I am going to go fishing is in someone else's pond.

And don't deceive yourself into believing that your customers are loyal to you. Your customers are loyal to themselves and their needs first. And if you do not meet their new and ever-changing needs by improving year after year on the value you provide them, they will painfully go to someone else that can provide it.

The 3 Day Entrepreneur understands that they need to continually improve or their business will die.

Conclusion

The 3 Day Entrepreneur continually seeks better ways to create even more value. They also look for better ways to use less time, effort, resources and money to generate that value. Lastly, they dedicate themselves to finding better ways to get high quality results that don't dependent on them. Ultimately, by improving in this way they will continue to reap greater and greater rewards both in time and money, and fully enjoy the free time that they value so highly.

PART III

The Lifestyle of the
3 Day Entrepreneur

It's now time to get into the nuts and bolts of the 3 Day Entrepreneur Lifestyle. It's time to look at what they do day-to-day, and what their routine looks like. It's also time to learn the practical ways you can create this lifestyle for yourself.

But before we do, I would like to introduce you to another special 3 Day Entrepreneur:

Danielle Julia Cuomo

Danielle Julia Cuomo is the owner of Virtual Assist USA, A Virtual Assistant firm that takes the ordinary VA experience and turns it into the extraordinary. She is another 3 Day Entrepreneur that has discovered the secret of working less than 30 hours a week, but still exceeding the 6 figure mark. This is what she has to say about the 3 Day Entrepreneur Lifestyle…

Danielle's Story

"When I first launched my business, I was no stranger to the all-nighters spent with my laptop and espresso. I knew that I was building a business and a dream, but I also knew that it wasn't sustainable nor healthy. I wanted to enjoy what I had worked so hard for, so in 2012, I put controls in place to work less.

What really made the difference and helped me work less, but still create a lot of value is when I got my own assistant. 10 years ago, assistants were only available to high level executives. Now, with virtual assistants, it's a practical decision to have someone assist with the time-consuming tasks like e-mail management, marketing and operations.

This is what I rely on to help my vision, for helping as many entrepreneurs as possible live out their dreams while working less, become a reality.

If I could give entrepreneur's out in the marketplace some advice on how to work less but still create outstanding value, I would say to realize that you can't do it all yourself. There is always someone out there who can do it better, faster or cheaper than you. It's a hard realization for any entrepreneur's like myself who are over-achievers. Once you put your ego behind you, it makes a world of a difference!"

CHAPTER

8

Ultimate Time Management: The 80/20 Task Manager

"A man who dares to waste one hour of time has not discovered the value of life."
Charles Darwin

We've spoken about focusing on the highest value tasks that bring the highest return of investment. We've also spoken about how there is always opportunity to leverage the use of our time, efforts, resources, and money in order to use less to achieve an even greater return. And, we discussed getting high quality results in a way that is not dependent on you, as well as how to continue to improve on our results.

But what does this practically look like in the daily life of the 3 Day Entrepreneur?

Not All Tasks are Created Equal

In a small business there are about 10,000 different tasks that you are required to do in order to make the business operate and be successful. Yet we would also agree that each of those different tasks carry a different level of value.

For example taking 30 minutes to go buy paperclips at the local office supply store has very different value compared to using that same 30 minutes to touch base with a high value potential client.

Yet, as obvious as this is, entrepreneurs have certain challenges that prevent them from focusing on the highest value tasks in their business. These are:

1. It is in our nature to be distracted by the overwhelming amount of things we have to do.

2. We tend to do the things that come naturally to us, and unfortunately those things are not always the most valuable.

3. We only have a limited amount of time to do anything.

So how does The 3 Day Entrepreneur overcome these obvious, but very huge obstacles to our productivity? The key is focus. The 3 Day Entrepreneur maximizes their profit potential by limiting themselves to only doing the tasks that produce the highest value. Everything else is delegated, automated, systematized, outsourced or eliminated.

So the first question The 3 Day Entrepreneur asks is:

"What are the tasks that bring the most value in an organization?"

In order to determine these, we first need to define what is considered "valuable," in a business.

What is "Valuable" in a Business?

Value in business is determined by:

1. The amount of revenue and profit that an activity generates.

2. The amount of equity (internal value) that it increases, and

3. How well the activity helps you more achieve your business vision.

For example, consider bookkeeping. If we were to do an assessment of the value of bookkeeping, using these criteria, what would we find?

- Revenue or profit the bookkeeping function generates: $0

- Equity that bookkeeping in itself builds in the business: $0

- Helping achieve the business vision: In itself, it helps only maintain things and keep them exactly where they are. So the answer is zero.

Therefore, according to our criteria, bookkeeping, though necessary, is not valuable.

Now, I know right now many of you (especially the bean counters) are crawling in your skin. But the reality is, unless it brings money, equity, or propels you the next level in your business, it is not valuable.

Now, is it necessary? The answer is yes. Which means that it needs to get done. But if it doesn't create value, then it cannot be done by the most valuable person in the business, which is you, the business owner.

Now let's consider something else, like creating a joint venture (JV) partnership with a high value referral partner. (A high value referral partner is someone who already brings you business, but in a JV relationship, they will exclusively work with you, and bring you much more business.)

So let's ask the questions again:

- How much profit does a high value JV generate? A whole lot.

- How much equity does high value JV in itself build in the business? A tremendous amount. By establishing a locked in strategy that will bring you more and more business for years to come, it substantially increases the equity in your business by a massive amount, especially when you are ready to sell.

- How much does it help you more achieve your business vision? If your vision includes being successful in your business then it will propel you the next level in your business very quickly.

Therefore, a joint venture relationship is extremely valuable and it, therefore, merits the business owner's undivided attention.

The 20%, 4%, and 1% Rule

Now let's refer back to the famous Pareto principle, also known as the 80/20 rule.

It says that in any group or organization, roughly 80% of the things you do bring 20% of the results, while 20% of the things you do bring 80% of the results.

And, if you were to take it further you would also find that while...

- 80% of the things you do bring 20% of the results and
- 20% of the things you do bring 80% of the results;
- 4% of the things you do bring 64% of the results* and
- 1% of the things you do bring 50% of the results**.

    * (20% of 20% is 4%, and 80% of 80% is 64%)
    **(20% of 20% of 20% is 1%, and 80% of 80% of 80% is approximately 50%)

Task Level	Input	Output
A	1%	50%
B	4%	64%
C	20%	80%
D	80%	20%

Now if you were to calculate what the return would be for each of these, you would see why focusing on high value tasks bring the greatest returns for your business. Let's look at our next example:

Task Level	Input	Output	Return
A	1%	50%	5000%
B	4%	64%	1600%
C	20%	80%	400%
D	80%	20%	25%

Looking at our table we see that:

- 80% tasks will bring you a 25% return for your efforts,

- 20% tasks will bring you a 400% return,

- 4% tasks will bring you a 1600% return, and

- 1% tasks will bring you a whopping 5000% return for your efforts!

And if we compare the impact of each group of tasks, we find:

Value	Input	Output	Return	Impact
A	1%	50%	5000%	200X
B	4%	64%	1600%	64X
C	20%	80%	400%	16X
D	80%	20%	25%	1X

Therefore the A level or 1% tasks have a 200X greater impact than the D Level or 80% tasks that take up a substantial amount of our time.

Now, imagine if you were to consistently accomplish A-level, high value tasks (the 1% that brings 50% of results) for the next 30 days. Where do you think your business will be?

From Will

 "My mentor, David Finkel of Maui Mastermind, taught me most of the concepts in this chapter. The one idea that stuck with me most was the concept of the magic 1% that brings 50% of the results. It is by far the greatest thing that has allowed me to create a 3 Day Entrepreneur Lifestyle for myself. I just determined that I would ONLY do the 20% that brought 80% of the results, with my goal being to eventually only do the 1% that brought 50% of results. The more and more I strove to hit that 1%, the more value I began to create, and the more time I began freeing up for myself. Because of this, I currently work about 1–2 days a week, and make 6 figures. My goal is in the next few years is to reach the 7 or 8 figure mark, but still working 1–2 days a week."

The Money Buckets

Another way to look at this is in terms of buckets.

Imagine 5 buckets labeled A–E that represent a group of tasks in your business, and each bucket has a certain value that each group of tasks you do brings.

Bucket	A	B	C	D	E
Value	$1M	$100K	$10K	$1K	$0

A Task Bucket—Tasks that bring $1M each
B Task Bucket—Tasks that bring $100K each
C Task Bucket—Tasks that bring $10K each
D Task Bucket—Tasks that bring $1K each
E Task Bucket—Tasks that bring $0 each

Where do typical entrepreneurs generally spend most of their time? Here is a common example:

Bucket	A	B	C	D	E
Value	$1M	$100K	$10K	$1K	$0
Where Entrepreneur Spends Time	0%	0%	5%	15%	80%

You'll notice something that's common to most entrepreneurs: they spend 80% of their time on the $0 column, and very little on everything else. And generally the first 2 columns are left untouched.

What kind of return do you think they will create if they operate like this for a whole year?

On the other hand, where do business investors and venture capitalists spend most of their time? Here is a common example:

Bucket	A	B	C	D	E
Value	$1M	$100K	$10K	$1K	$0
Where Entrepreneur Spends Time	0%	0%	5%	15%	80%
Where Investors Spends Time	80%	15%	5%	0%	0%

Most successful business builders, business investors, venture capitalists, and the 3 Day entrepreneur will use 80–90% of his or her time in the 6, 7 and 8 figure+ columns while avoiding the $0 column like the plague.

Exercise

1. Take out a sheet of paper and draw 5 buckets labeled A–E, and label each bucket as either $1M, $100K, $10K, $1K, $0.

2. Consider your last week. List 10 of the activities you spent the most time on in your business.

3. Answer the following questions:

   • What percentage of activities you spent time on last week brought, or will bring you $1M or more?

   • What percentage of activities you spent time on last week brought, or will bring you $100K or more?

   • What percentage of activities you spent time on last week brought, or will bring you $10K or more?

   • What percentage of activities you spent time on last week brought, or will bring you $1K or more?

   • What percentage of activities you spent time on last week brought, or will bring you $0?

4. Now looking at where you spend the majority of your time, does it give you a better picture of why your business is where it is at, and why you are getting the return on investment that you are currently getting?

Conclusion

No tasks are created equal. There are a special category of tasks that bring the vast majority of results in a business. If a person can focus on only doing the tasks that bring the greatest value in terms of revenue, equity, and achieving one's vision, it is only a matter of time until you begin to reap the rewards of the 3 Day Entrepreneur Lifestyle.

Now let us look at what the highest value tasks in a business look like…

CHAPTER

9

Getting High Value Tasks Done

"I am like a mosquito in a nudist camp; I know what I want to do, but I don't know where to begin."
Stephen Bayne

How does the 3 Day Entrepreneur consistently focus on doing the high value tasks in his or her organization?

Here is a list of the 3 things that the 3 Day Entrepreneur does to consistently accomplish the tasks that result in massive value for the business:

1. **Identify the tasks that truly create value for your business.**
2. **Leverage them up to magnify their value.**
3. **Make sure they consistently get done.**

Step 1—Identifying High Valued Tasks in Your Organization

There are 2 types of high value tasks in an organization:

1. **General business high value tasks**—Found in almost every business, these bring substantial value to an organization.

2. **Specific business high valued tasks**—These are the things specific to your industry that you have already done in your business, which have brought, and will continue to bring your business a substantial amount of value.

General High Value Tasks—"The Big 6"

General High Value Tasks produce the highest return in terms of revenue, equity, and attaining the business vision.

Since 70-80% of businesses are relatively the same, these tasks tend to be the tasks that produce valuable returns across most businesses.

Here is a general list of the "Big 6" tasks that bring the greatest value to a business:

1. **Developing highly profitable ideas.**

2. **Developing relationships with high value people (i.e.: referral relationships, high net-worth clients, joint ventures, centers of influence, funding sources, etc.)**

3. **Building high powered teams.**

4. **Creating profitable products or systems that generate revenue over and over again.**

5. **Creating or finding valuable opportunities that can multiply your value and create greater leverage.**

6. **Creating breakthroughs that greatly multiply the positive results you are getting in your business.**

For a complete list of all of the general high value tasks in a business go to www.the3dayentrepreneur.com/resources.

The Big 6 tasks are so valuable for your business that they tend to fall into the category of the 1% that bring 50% of the results in your business. Because of this, the 3 Day Entrepreneur makes sure he or she does as many Big 6 tasks as they can every week. If you can imagine this, consider what your business would look like if you just got one Big 6 task accomplished every week for a whole year. It will completely change the face of your business.

Exercise

1. Make a list of Big 6 opportunities you can create in your business.

2. Create a routine so that you get one Big 6 task done every week.

3. Keep track every month of how you did, celebrate, and then improve on it.

Specific High Value Tasks

Specific High Value Tasks are tasks you've discovered through your efforts, which produce great value in your business and industry.

Exercise

Since specific high value tasks are those that you have experience with and have discovered on your own, a good exercise is to take inventory of what these may be.

1. Take a moment to list the tasks that you do or have done, that have brought your business the most value in the past.

2. Write down the amount of long-term revenue or equity that these tasks have brought, or will bring to your organization.

3. List more ways that you can do these task more consistently in your business.

Both the general and specific task lists are where the 3 Day Entrepreneur focuses 80% of their time and energy. This is how you can have a greater impact that results in creating more value while using less time and effort.

Step 2—Leveraging High Value Tasks and Boosting their Value

As we learned earlier, there are always opportunities to redesign a task to produce substantially greater value, while using less time, effort, resources, and money (TERM).

For example, here are ways to leverage Big 6 general high value tasks:

- Instead of developing highly profitable ideas, mastermind with a highly creative and successful group of people, and together come up with an abundance of profitable ideas for you.

- Instead of building highly profitable relationships, lock in a joint venture contract to be the sole provider for a high producing referral source.

- Instead of coming up with breakthrough ideas for improving the ROI for a profitable product or service, select, train, and develop powerful teams to do it for you.

- Instead of selecting, training, and developing your own power team, hire an effective CEO that can lead and develop your power team for you.

For the 3 Day Entrepreneur, boosting the value of a high value tasks is a matter of asking the Value, Leverage, and Automation questions for each task that needs to be done. If they are not able to find ways to boost the value of a task, they leverage their team to help them find the answers. All this brain power inevitably results in finding new solutions.

Exercise

1. Take all of the specific high value tasks from the previous exercise and reflect on new ways that you can get a greater result from them (If you cannot think of any, ask your team.)

2. Now come up with ways that you can get that greater result using less time, effort, resources, and money (Again, use your team to help you find solutions.)

3. Calculate how much more revenue the new scaled up versions of these tasks can bring you.

4. Test one of your new ideas and evaluate the results.

From this exercise, you can see how much more value you can create when you spend the time coming up with ways to boost the impact of high value tasks even further.

Step 3—Getting High Valued Tasks Done

Now that we have identified the high value tasks, we need to find ways to do them on a consistent basis.

Here is a list of ways the 3 Day Entrepreneur uses to get high value tasks done on daily, weekly, and monthly basis.

1. **Label all of your tasks as A, B, C, D, and E tasks as discussed earlier. Focus all of your time on the A, B and C tasks while delegating, deferring, deleting, or automating your D and E tasks.**

   - Delegate—To your team, assistants, virtual assistants, personal assistants, etc.

   - Defer—Wait, the tasks may resolve themselves in time.

   - Delete—Eliminate them all together (Do we really need to answer email every day? Do we really need to email back to say "thank you")?

   - Automate—Create an automated process that will eliminate your need for fulfilling D and E activities.

   For a complete list of general business A, B, C, D, and E tasks go to www.the3dayentpreneur.com/resources.

2. **Eliminate your D and E tasks, and all that you will have left is A, B, and C tasks to do.**

   Once you eliminate the less valuable tasks from your to do list, you can focus all your attention on the valuable tasks that are left.

   For a complete list of 100+ Ways to Maximize Your Time By Eliminating Unnecessary Tasks go to www.the3dayentpreneur.com/resources.

3. **Be determined to do at least 2 or 3 A-level tasks daily.**

Out of the all the things you have to do during the day, make sure 3 of them are A level tasks, and that you do these first.

This way, even if you focus all of the rest of your day on B, C, D even E tasks, it won't matter.

4. **Pick a day during the week (or few hours) to focus only on accomplishing the highest valuable tasks in your week.**

If you get 5–6 A level tasks done in one day—what you do the rest of the week won't matter.

From Will

 By picking 1–2 days during the week, and burning through 5–6 high value tasks in those days, every week, I eventually realized that I did not need to work any other days. This is how I was able to reduce my schedule to a 1 or 2 day workweek.

---

5. **Get your highest value tasks done first thing in the morning.** If you don't get around to everything else on your schedule, it won't matter as much.

6. **Schedule your highest value tasks when you are at your best during the day, and get them done.** This is the time of day when you are usually in the zone.

7. **Use the Pomodoro Technique.** Pick your high value tasks, and limit yourself to spending no more than 25 minutes per task. If a task will take longer, limit yourself to 25 minute additional increments until the task is complete. Remember Parkinson's Law!

Time Killers—How to Free Up an Extra 5–10 Hours of Your Week Immediately

Below is a list of time killers that you can get rid of right now, which will immediately free up an extra 5–10 hours in your schedule every week:

1. **Reading emails**—Checking your email more than 2–3 times a day is generally wasted time. Commit to checking emails only 2–3 times a day. Once in morning, once in midday and once before you leave work.

2. **Checking texts**—Checking your texts more than 2–3 times a day generally leads to more wasted time as well. Commit to checking text only 2–3 times a day. Once in morning, once in midday and once before you leave work.

3. **Traveling**—With all the new technology today, we don't have to waste time traveling as much anymore. Sometimes by having customers come to the office, or meeting with them on a conference call or video chat, can save us many hours of travel time.

4. **Double work**—You would be amazed at how much time we spend doing things 2–3 times, or more, unnecessarily, because we are in the habit of doing this. Train yourself to do things once, and only once.

5. **Repeatedly picking up a paper or viewing an email**—We also tend to pick up papers multiple times before we ever do anything about it. Make a commitment to only pick up a piece of paper once, and do something about it. Or if it is electronic, make up your mind to only read an email or text, or electronic document once, and then take action on it immediately.

6. **Multitasking**—Multitasking is a great way to get a lot of things done, if you want to take a lot of time doing it. Because of the constant shifting of your mind from one task to the next, you sometimes have

to think through things again and again just to remember what you were doing. Pick one thing you need to do and get it done. Then focus on the next.

7. **Allowing Disruptions**—If you allow yourself to be disrupted, it takes 2–3 times longer to finish what you start. And statistically we generally get interrupted about 40 times a day! You can do the math and realize how much time we are wasting by allowing ourselves to be interrupted. Set yourself in an environment where you will not be disrupted. Turn off the phone, close down your email, shut the door and get your work done.

8. **Social Media**—Though it is a great tool for business, it is not effective if your time is not focused. Make a commitment to spend no more than 15–30 minutes a day on social media for business and no more, because 3 posts a day should be plenty to stay in touch with your customers and prospects.

9. **Lack of Time Boundaries**—When we do tasks, if we don't set a limit of how much time we will spend, Parkinson's Law says that we will take as much time as possible. Follow the Pomodoro Technique and set a 25 minute time limit on all the tasks you need to accomplish. Try to get the task done in 25 minutes. If not, give yourself another 25 minutes to accomplish it, and so on...

10. **Surfing the Internet**—Though I know not many business people do this, but for the ones that do, much time can be wasted on surfing the web. If you are going to surf, set a time limit of 15–30 minutes or less of surfing per day.

11. **False Starts**—Many of us start the day not knowing what we will do. We therefore spend anywhere from 1–2 hours just getting ourselves organized to start the day. You can imagine how much wasted time that produces. Spend 20–30 minutes at the end of each business day doing a quick review and setting up your to do

list for the following day. Take 15 minutes to review it the following day, and get started on your work!

12. **Bottomless To Do List**—Having a daily To Do list with 25+ things will probably overwhelm anyone. We waste a lot of time trying to get everything done. Pick no more than 5 things to do per day: 3 high value items and 2 others tasks of your choosing.

13. **Working at Home**—You would be surprised how much busy work we bring home that can get done just as well if we did it at the office. Home time is supposed to be devoted to your family. Therefore make it so! Make a decision that you will no longer bring any work home; leave work at work. If you work at home, set undisturbed office hours, and when they are finished, spend time with the family.

14. **Entertainment**—This is more a family time killer than a business one. But I wanted to put it here because the time we spend glued to the TV, or doing other recreational activities, is often time we can be spending with our loved ones. Make a choice to either do away with the TV altogether or limit your entertainment activities to 1–2 days a week. 2 hours a day of television equals 14 hours a week that you can give back to your family.

Conclusion

You can experience the 3 Day Entrepreneur lifestyle and make more and more money by:

- Only focusing on the 20%, 4% or 1% of tasks that bring the highest return;
- by leveraging them up so that they produce an even greater return,
- and by making sure they get done on a daily, weekly, and monthly basis.

CHAPTER

10

Constant Evaluation and Improvement

"When we deal in generalities, we shall never succeed. When we deal in specifics, we shall rarely have a failure. When performance is measured, performance improves. When performance is measured and reported, the rate of performance accelerates."

Thomas S Monson

The principle of Kaizen states there is always room for improvement, and people have a natural tendency to waste valuable resources. The 3 Day Entrepreneur sets up their schedule to take advantage of improvements that can greatly boost their ROI. They're also on the lookout for more ways to reduce waste by shaving off more unnecessary use of time, effort, resources, and money.

The 3 Day Entrepreneur does this by creating an environment of continual improvement. The goal is to create greater value, while minimizing wasted resources. This is why the 3 Day Entrepreneur sets up a daily, weekly, and monthly planning and review time. By making time to evaluate their decisions and actions, they can keep improving them.

The Daily Plan

The 3 Day Entrepreneur sets up a 15–25 minute time at the beginning of the day to plan out the day's activities. This is done in order to make sure they consistently do the tasks that bring the most value for their business. The 3 Day Entrepreneur does this by asking themselves the following set of questions, every day.

Daily Planning Questions

1. What are the most valuable things I can do today?

   - Choose 3 A-Level activities to do for the day, and put a potential dollar amount that you will make by accomplishing them.

2. How can I do them in a way that will use the least amount of time, effort, resources and money (TERM)?

3. How can I multiply the value of these tasks even further?

4. How can I get them done, without it being dependent on me?

5. (My favorite) How can I get these tasks done in a way that is fun for me?

By planning the day this way, you set your focus and plan your actions so that you end the day with a lot more value than when you started.

The Daily Review

The 3 Day Entrepreneur also sets up a 15–25 minute time at the end of every day to review the decisions and actions made that day. The purpose is to identify opportunities to create greater value for the next day, leverage their time, effort, and resources better, and further automate their system.

At the end of a typical workday, the 3 Day Entrepreneur asks the following questions.

Daily Review Questions

1. How much value did I create today? (Put a dollar amount to it)

2. What could I have done differently so that I could have created even greater value?

3. How could I have gotten the same or better result using less TERM?

4. How could I have more effectively automated the process?

5. How am I going to put the improvements I discovered into practice tomorrow?

By making improvements on a daily basis, The 3 Day Entrepreneur is able to quickly adjust their aim so that they get closer and closer to the bull's-eye: their goal of getting the greatest value for their efforts.

For a template to do your own 3 Day Entrepreneur Daily Plan and Review go to www.3DayEntrepreneur.com/resources.

The Weekly Plan and Review

The weekly review is a 1–2 hour session that focuses on stepping back and reviewing the results of all the efforts made during the week. The 3 Day Entrepreneur looks at the results he or she accomplished in all of the major "Big 6" areas that produce the most value for the organization. They do this by answering the following high value questions.

Value Review and Planning Questions

1. High Value Ideas

- What valuable ideas did I create this week?

- What is the potential or actual ($) return on investment I got from it?

- What valuable ideas can I create this coming week?

2. High Value Relationships

- What valuable relationships did I establish or develop this week?

- What is the potential or actual ($) return on investment I got from it?

- What valuable relationships can I start or develop this coming week?

3. High Value Team

- What valuable team member did I add or develop this week?

- What is the potential or actual ($) return on investment I got from it?

- What valuable team member can I add or develop this coming week?

4. High Value Systems

- What valuable system did I create or develop this week?
- What is the potential or actual ($) return on investment I got from it?
- What valuable system can I create or develop this coming week?

5. High Value Opportunities

- What valuable opportunities did I discover and take advantage of this week?
- What is the potential or actual ($) return on investment I got from it?
- What valuable opportunities can I take advantage of or develop this coming week?

6. High Value Breakthroughs

- What valuable breakthroughs did I make this week?
- What is the potential or actual ($) return on investment I got from it?
- What valuable breakthroughs can I make this coming week?

By stepping back and evaluating how much value was created during the week, the 3 Day Entrepreneur is able to stay focused on creating the most optimal results for their business week per week. Also, he or she will be able to plan out the following week, by anticipating all of the A-level tasks and opportunities, and making sure they get accomplished.

Exercise

1. Take a moment to reflect on your last week and answer all of the Value Creation Review Questions.

2. How much value did you create last week?

3. If you continue having weeks like this, will it help you succeed like you want to?

4. What changes are you going to make for the following week?

For a template to conduct your own 3 Day Entrepreneur Weekly Review go to www.3DayEntrepreneur.com/resources.

The Monthly Review

The monthly review is an evaluation of all of the collective efforts done during the month to see how well all those efforts and improvements were able to accomplish the monthly goals originally set. Since it is an overview of hundreds of efforts made throughout the month, it is approached in a more general way.

Here, the 3 Day Entrepreneur spends a few hours reviewing the Daily and Weekly Review exercises as well as focusing on the big picture goals for the month.

The idea is to evaluate not only if the target goals were achieved for the month, but how well they were achieved. The 3 Day Entrepreneur is always seeking a better, faster, and greater approach to reaching goals.

Below is a list of the type of questions the 3 Day Entrepreneur asks to evaluate their efforts every month so that they can improve their systems for the future.

WWW, WDW, and WDD

The purpose of the monthly review is to identify all of the major areas that have brought the most value, the areas that are not working as anticipated, and areas that need improvement. The 3 Day Entrepreneur refers to these as the WWW, WDW, and the WDD.

1. **WWW**—What went well?
2. **WDW**—What did not go well?
3. **WDD**—What will be done differently?

The idea is that the 3 Day Entrepreneur brainstorms and lists as many answers to these three questions as possible. Once you finish, you can take pride in how well things went the past month (WWW). You can take a critical eye to the areas that did not go as well (WDW). Lastly, you can put together a game plan to do things better next month, so that you can reach all of your major goals (WDD).

The Monthly Goal Review

After the quick WWW, WDW, and WDD review, the 3 Day Entrepreneur gets more specific to see how well they were about to accomplish their goals. Here are some typical questions you can ask:

1. What were the Goals this past month?
2. Did I achieve my goals? Why or why not? (Go through each goal).
3. How much ROI did I generate from achieving these goals?
4. What could I have done differently so that I could have achieved a greater ROI?

5. What could I have done differently to get the same or better result using less TERM?

6. How could I have automated this system better?

Uses this information to evaluate how effective you were in achieving your goals, as well as looking forward to improve and do even better in the next month.

Choosing the "One Big Thing"

Choosing the "One Big Thing" is based on the idea there are really valuable "big steps" that one can take that will greatly speed up the process of accomplishing your vision and goals. The 3 Day Entrepreneur makes the effort to find out what those big steps are, and then focuses on accomplishing at least "One Big Thing" a month. We do this by first answering the "One Big Thing" question:

> **What "One Big Thing" can I accomplish this month that will greatly speed up the process of getting me closer to my vision?**

The "One Big Thing" takes priority over everything else. This is because if you don't get everything done that you wanted to for the month, at least you did the "One Big Thing" that will propel your business the farthest.

Every month the 3 Day Entrepreneur goes over how well they did in getting their "One Big Thing" done for the month. They do this in order to make improvements that will push their business to a higher level, each and every month.

Exercise

1. Take a moment and ask yourself, "What One Big Thing can I accomplish in the next month that will really speed up the process of seeing my vision become a reality this year?"

2. Come up with a plan to accomplish that "One Big Thing" next month.

3. Tell someone you trust to hold you accountable to accomplishing that "One Big Thing" in the next 30 days.

For a template to conduct your own 3 Day Entrepreneur Monthly Review go to www.3DayEntrepreneur.com/resources.

Conclusion

The 3 Day Entrepreneur is dedicated to continual improvement, which will greatly increase their ROI. We do this by creating daily, weekly, and monthly reviews that we can use to measure and improve our progress. By gathering this information, the 3 Day Entrepreneur is constantly able to set better plans in motion, and move closer to their target. This allows us to be fully prepared to attack any project or business with a powerful plan and a thorough expectation of success.

CHAPTER
11

Creating a Success Routine

"The secret of your future is hidden in your daily routine."

Mike Murdock

Up to now we've discussed how the 3 Day Entrepreneur primarily focuses on identifying high value tasks and doing them. We've even discussed how the 3 Day Entrepreneur continually improves in order to create more value and leverage that result for a greater ROI. Now we will look out how the 3 Day Entrepreneur puts it all together in a typical workweek in their lives.

The 3 Day Entrepreneur Schedule

Before we begin to discuss the 3 Day Entrepreneur routine, let's discuss the biggest question that is probably on your mind while you are reading this book. That is,

> "How in the world do I get everything done in less than 3 days a week?"

Well, from what we have discussed so far, we can see how the 3 Day Entrepreneur gets much more done in less time than the typical entrepreneur. This is because the 3 Day Entrepreneur only chooses to do what is the most valuable and most leveraged tasks that bring the highest result. But couldn't the 3 Day Entrepreneur also fall into the trap of doing high value tasks every hour of every day of the week?

The answer is yes. But this is where the 3 Day Entrepreneur sets up boundaries to prevent themselves from working too hard or too much, even if the work is highly rewarding.

Shaving Off Two Days a Week

It is said that in 1519 the Spanish conquistador Hernando Cortez was able to overthrow the great Mexican empire with only a handful of men. How did he do it? He burned his ship. He gave his men no other option but to conquer and survive. By removing their option for failure, it motivated them to succeed.

Though harsh, it is a great example of Parkinson's Law at work. In the same way, the 3 Day Entrepreneur is able to work 3 days or less because they create an environment that makes it impossible for them to fail. How do they do it? They simply make the decision to only go to work on 3 days. On every other day, they hang up the phone, they don't answer email, they ignore all texts, and they do everything else but work.

What does this do? Like Parkinson's law says, eventually you will find creative ways of getting everything that needs to get done accomplished in the 3 days that you have to work. You continue to make money, your customers continue to be satisfied, and the business continues to run when you are not there.

Exercise

This is an exercise in courage, but if you do it, you will see first-hand how you can live the 3 Day Entrepreneur Lifestyle.

1. Look at your schedule and pick one day that you will no longer work (or just pick 8–10 hours in your weekly schedule you will no longer work)

2. Do absolutely no work on that day (or 8–10 hour time slot). Do this for an entire month.

How did the business get along without you the first week? How about the Second? Third? How about the Fourth?
What new things did you learn from this exercise?

From Will

 I originally started working the 3 Day Entrepreneur Lifestyle as part of a dare. I dared myself to not work on Mondays or Fridays, but instead to spend those days with my family. It forced me to get really creative on the 3 days that I was working. I won't lie, there were many apologies, and a few nail-biting close calls. However, next thing I knew, after a month had passed, my customers were happy, I was getting paid, and I also had plenty of time to spend with the family. This was also the month that my income doubled as well...

The 3 Day Entrepreneur Success Routine

Successful people continue to create great success year after year because they do successful things day after day. They are creatures of habit that will rarely change their routine, especially if it is bringing them millions of dollars!

The 3 Day Entrepreneur creates a success routine by piecing together the right tasks, actions, resources, and efforts in such a way that combined, it consistently produces a profitable result.

What should we put in our day? Generally, create a routine from the 4 specific areas that bring the greatest value to your business. These are:

1. Doing only the high level tasks that create the most value. (20% that brings 80% of the results)

2. Implementing the best practices that produce the best results in your industry.

3. Focusing on constant improvement and self-development.

4. Taking consistent breaks to rest, have fun, spend time with family, recharge batteries, etc.

Exercise

1. Take out a sheet of paper or pull out your laptop, and write down what your typical daily routine is (or if you don't have one, just write down what you did yesterday).

2. Calculate how much money your daily routine has brought you or will bring you in the future.

3. Ask yourself, if you continue with this same routine for a whole year, how much value will you create?

4. Now rearrange your routine, so that the only things you do in your day come from the 4 areas the 3 Day Entrepreneur focuses on (I.e.: high value tasks, best practices, continual improvement, rest, etc.)

5. Calculate how much money your new routine will bring you.

6. Ask yourself, if you continue with this new routine for a whole year, how much value will you create?

Adopting Your New Routine

Though it is challenging to adopt a new routine, the truth is it is more painful to continue the old one. Since you are going to follow a routine either way, why not train yourself to follow a routine that will bring you a 6 or 7 figure income, and more time to enjoy your life?

So, the best way to train in your new routine is to either:

1. Bite the bullet and follow your new success routine for 30 days until it becomes a habit. Or,

2. Once a month, add one valuable thing to your current routine, as well as take out one thing that is not valuable. After 12 months you will have a completely new and successful routine that will bring you many rewards.

From Will

 I have found that the following routine has brought me the most growth both in my life and in my business. It is also the routine that helped me double my income in a year, and cut my work time to only 1–2 days a week. Whenever I add any of these elements in my day, I see the rewards. The more elements I add from this list, the more rewards I see...

1. **Ask my daily focus questions**—5 minutes

   • What am I happy about?
   • What am I grateful for?

- What am I excited about?
- How can I fulfill my purpose in life today?

2. **Read my bible** — 15–25 minutes

3. **Daily gratitude** — 5 minutes

4. **Prayer** — 10 minutes (Short I know, but if its short I can do it daily)

5. **Self-development Exercises** — 15–25 minutes

6. **Visualization exercise** — 10 minutes

7. **Book writing** — 15–25 minutes

8. **Review my daily plan** — 15 minutes

9. **Check and respond to important emails and texts** — 15–25 minutes

10. **Do my A-level tasks for the day** — 25–50 minutes each (with breaks in between each)

11. **Meetings with High Value People** — 25–50 minutes each.

12. **Entrepreneur Idea Development** — 25 minutes

13. **Wealth Building** — 25 minutes

14. **Reading for Personal Development** — 25 minutes

15. **Breaks** — Either rest break, meal breaks, family breaks, or fun breaks, I litter my day with breaks to recharge my batteries.

Conclusion

The 3 Day Entrepreneur is able to consistently create great value because we create great value on a daily basis. We do this by consistently doing the highest value tasks, implementing best practices, through constant self-development, and taking breaks to recharge on a daily basis. Even though the 3 Day Entrepreneur could work every day, we set boundaries to create the most possible value in the shortest amount of time.

PART IV

Turning Your Current Business into a 3 Day Entrepreneur Business

Now we will take all we've learned about the 3 day Entrepreneur mindset, and lifestyle and see how we can apply these to create a 6 or 7 figure business, working less than 3 days a week.

To start, in business, the 3 Day Entrepreneur's biggest focus is optimization. Optimization is the ability to create the greatest possible result in every area of your business. This is possible because in every business, in any industry, you will find best practices that combine the right efforts, the right resources, in the right sequence, to create the highest possible result for that business.

You can see this best when you look at the corporate giants that dominate the marketplace. Giants like Wal-Mart and McDonalds have identified the optimal systems that create value upon value, year after year for their stockholders.

You also notice this trend in the large franchises in the world today. As a matter of fact, out of the 3500 franchises in the United States, as of the writing of this book, combined have a failure rate of only 7%. This means that 93% of franchises accomplish their mission of producing increasing profit and value for the owner. Why? Because they have identified the optimal systems for their marketing, sales, customer satisfaction, operations, financial, team and leadership areas.

In other words, the 3 Day Entrepreneur is not interested in marketing to get a customer; we are interested in finding the optimal marketing strategy that will bring thousands of customers to the business. The 3 Day Entrepreneur is not interested in making one sale, but in creating an optimal sales system, that helps convert hundreds of leads into customers.

In this section, we will learn how the 3 Day entrepreneur uses optimal systems in the business to create a 6 or 7 figure income, while working less than 3 days a week. We will focus on the following major business pillars that create the most value in a business:

The Value Creators
- Marketing, and Sales

The Value Multipliers

- Pricing, Increasing Customer ROI, and Additional Profit Centers

The Value Sustainers

- Leadership and Team

- Finance

- Operations

But before we jump into the nuts and bolts, I would like to introduce you to another special person that has mastered the art of 3 Day Entrepreneurship...

J. Massey

J. Massey is a successful real estate investor with over 300 residential and commercial properties in his portfolio. He operates his real estate investing business working at most 5–10 hours a week. With his extra time he trains and develops real estate investors with his landmark program, Cash Flow Diary.

J. Massey's Story

Through a series of life—altering events, including the serious illness of his then-pregnant wife, an accident that left J. with a punctured lung that excluded him from being able to work, and even losing his family home—J. learned quickly that he had to change his mindset if he wanted to survive and thrive. He immediately took action, immersing himself into intensive real estate investor training. He hasn't looked back and has built a booming investing business, using very little of his own cash or credit.

Here is what J. had to say when asked how he is able to manage such a large amount of properties through the US, and globally, in only 5–10 hours a week:

"The key to my success is having a great team. I have an executive assistant, operations manager, and a CFO. All of the property managers report to the operations manager, and she takes care of everything. Whatever she is not authorized to handle, I handle, which is very little so the really big stuff she brings to me—but it doesn't happen all of the time.

On the real estate constructions side, under the operation manager there is a construction manager, and under him is the general contractor. So even on the rehab stuff, like if materials don't show, etc., I don t have to do anything because that is their job. They know construction better than I do. I truly believe you have to let people do what they do best, and only what they do best.

I also believe that the reason entrepreneurs get stressed out is that they try to do things they don't do best, because they think it's worth saving the money…It's not..

Then my CFO comes into play. I don't do accounting best. I don't do expense management best. I don't do budgeting and cash flow planning best. It's not my job. I let her do that. She also has a person that works with her because it eventually becomes too much for one person.

I don't do any of the things that I don't do best. And therefore that means there is a lot I don't do. Which leads me to only do the things that I do best."

CHAPTER 12

The Optimal Marketing Strategy

> "The aim of marketing is to make selling superfluous."
> **Peter Drucker**

When it comes to marketing, the 3 Day Entrepreneur does not market to get a customer. Instead, we market for the purpose of identifying something called the Optimal Marketing Strategy (OMS).

The Optimal Marketing Strategy is the right formula of marketing efforts, timing and spending that results in getting the greatest amount of qualified customers. These are the kind of customers that value what you are offering, will pay the prices you ask, and will continue to buy from you again and again.

The 3 Day Entrepreneur understands that every business has an optimal marketing strategy. All one has to do is to look at the most successful companies in your industry. The OMS is the reason the most successful competitors in your industry became the giants that they are.

Now once you identify the OMS for your industry, you can easily implement it yourself, and get the results that your most successful competitors are getting. Even better, you can automate the OMS to the point that the business never has to worry about getting customers ever again.

So, how do you find the Optimal Marketing Strategy of your business? The Optimal Marketing Strategy of a business can be found by looking at three areas:

1. **What's working for successful competitors;**
2. **What has worked in the past for your business; and**
3. **What always works.**

What's Working for Competitors

When identifying the OMS, the 3 Day Entrepreneur looks first to their competition. And not just any competition, but the competitors that are highly successful in the market place. Why? Because they have identified their optimal marketing strategy and are using it effectively.

Here are some good places that the 3 Day Entrepreneur looks to find out what their competitors are doing:

1. **Internet search**—The most successful businesses are usually spotlighted by different industry journals and blogs, and many articles are written about them.

2. **Books**—If you do a search for "How to Effectively Market a _____ _____ Business," usually the industry leaders have written a best-selling book that you can get all of their secrets from.

3. **Contact Them Directly**—Call a successful competitor's CEO, president, vice president of marketing, etc. and ask them for advice. As scary as this sounds, usually highly successful companies do not see

you as a threat, but they find significance in helping you get ahead. The only way to know is to ask.

Exercise

1. Make a list of the most successful competitors in your industry.

2. Do research on them to identify their Optimal Marketing Strategy. Either research online, read their book, or call them directly.

3. Take 1 or 2 simple ideas from their marketing playbook, and put it into practice for the next month.

4. Track your results, and improve them as time goes on.

What Has Worked in the Past

After attaining a steady flow of customers, the 3 Day Entrepreneur religiously tracks all of the sources of their customers through various methods. This is because they are on the hunt for their optimal marketing strategy.

Tracking shows you exactly where the customers are coming from, and gives you an idea for where the future customers will keep coming from. Tracking also gives you an idea of the source of your highest qualified customers, so that you can focus your efforts on building a business with the most valuable clients.

For example, suppose you get 20 customers from your advertising, and they are worth $100 each. You've made $2000. But, you also find that a certain referral partner relationship has also given you 10 customers, and these are worth $400 each. These have brought $4000. By tracking the marketing, you can see where your best customers are coming from, and determine where to put the majority of your efforts.

Also, the 3 Day Entrepreneur knows that since it costs $50 for each customer received through advertising, but it cost nothing for each referral received from the referral partner (an unlimited ROI)—it really motivates the 3 Day Entrepreneur to focus his or her efforts where it really counts.

Determining Your Marketing ROI

Here is a quick exercise to determine which of your marketing efforts are working and which ones are not:

1. Make a list of all the marketing efforts you used to get customers in the last 12 months

2. For each marketing effort, write down how much money you have made (customers you acquired) from each one.

3. Write down how much money you spent for each marketing effort to get each of those customers in the last 12 months.

4. Calculate your ROI with the following formula:

$$(Revenue) - (Marketing\ Expense)/$$
$$(Marketing\ Expense) \times 100\% = ROI$$

5. See what marketing efforts provide you with the biggest ROI, and build them up.

6. See what marketing efforts give you the lowest ROI and either make changes to improve them or get rid of them.

For a template to do a complete marketing ROI assessment go to www.the3dayentrepreneur.com/resources.

What Always Works

The 3 Day Entrepreneur also looks at the best marketing practices, which have historically worked over and over again, for all businesses, no matter what the industry. They first start testing their marketing strategies with these best marketing practices, and make improvements along the way.

The purpose, again, is to identify the optimal marketing strategy of the business, without spending a lot of time doing it.

Here are a few of the 3 Day Entrepreneur marketing tactics that tend to always work in almost any industry:

1. **Referrals**—Proactively asking current customers for introduction to people just like themselves. They key word is "proactive." You won't have new customers if you don't ask.

2. **Referral Partners**—These are other business people that are going after your target market, who do not compete against you. You can exchange referrals, provide a referral fee for each referral, or exchange resources.

3. **Cold Calling**—Cold calling is when you call potential customers you've never met before to establish trust that can later lead to an appointment. Sending a direct mail piece or an introductory email helps turn a cold call into a warm call, and makes it much easier to get results.

4. **Warm Calling**—Use your affiliation to a group or association as a way to get in front of your target audience (I.e.: Chamber of Commerce, etc.). Once they recognize you are a member of their "inner circle," appointments are much easier to get.

5. **Public Speaking**—Speak in front of a captive audience of your target market. This is extremely effective because it gives you expert status, which easily leads to more sales.

6. **Networking**—Meet up with like-minded business people to create more referral partner relationships that can send you business.

7. **Signs**—Post signs that capture the attention of people on the go. Historically signs have one of the highest ROIs in marketing.

8. **Center of Influence Network (COINS)**—These are influential individuals who can open doors to more opportunities by helping

connect you with a massive amount of your target customer. These are also the kind of people that can open doors you could never get in yourself.

9. **Internet Marketing**—Having a website, or multiple landing pages on the first page of search engines, either through using search engine optimization (SEO), pay per click, or social media makes it easier for your customers to find you. It also increases the awareness of your brand.

10. **Direct Marketing**—This is where you send fliers, postcards, letters, etc. through the mail, or by email, directly to a highly targeted audience. Direct mail has historically brought companies billions of dollars in revenue, and is still highly effective.

11. **Advertising**—Create an emotionally compelling ad, and put it in a magazine, newspaper, radio, and television that is read or viewed by your target audience. A well designed ad helps you generate thousands of new customers, without doing any additional work.

12. **Trade shows, Sponsorships**—Go to a tradeshow that is full of your target market, or rent a table or booth at an event full of your target market. This tactic has a high return rate and gets you easy prospects, and more sales.

13. **Group Marketing**—Group marketing is an exceedingly effective way to get a consistent flow of new customers. It involves finding a group, offline or online, that is full of your target market, and getting involved in it. Once in the group, you serve them by providing them valuable resources and information for free. Eventually you gain expert status in the group, and they will immediately think of you when they are ready to buy.

Exercise

1. Pick 3–4 Marketing Tactics for the previous list that always work.

2. Begin consistently doing this marketing tactic daily for the next 30 days.

3. Track your results.

4. At the end of 30 days, evaluate your results. Keep the marketing tactics that worked, replace the ones that did not.

---

3 Simple Ways to Get Your Marketing Done for Free

Marketing is essential for your small business, because without it, you have no business. But if cash is tight, and you don't have the time, what can you do to market your business? Here are a couple of ways to get the marketing your business needs done, using very little of your time, and without spending a dime on marketing:

1. Ask your marketing company to give you their services for free.

If you need to market your services, other people need it too. Negotiate with your marketing company to give you free services if you refer them a certain number of customers. Start referring like crazy, and you'll get your marketing for free.

I got a free website, following this particular strategy.

2. Get your customers to pay for your marketing.

Like I said, other people need marketing too. Find a quality marketing company that offers their services dirt cheap (you may have to go to another state or country). Then double the price and sell it as an added service to your customers or the public.

You only have to sell it to one customer, and your marketing will be paid for. If you sell it to more people, you will have an additional stream of income.

I got all of my SEO, email marketing, video marketing, and social media marketing free following this strategy. I also started my own SEO business, and created a nice additional stream of income for myself.

3. Hire a virtual assistant and have your customers or business partners pay for it.

Virtual assistants (VA) are the Swiss army knives of the business world. They can do just about anything, and do it inexpensively. If you pool some business owners together who need a virtual assistant to do their marketing, ask the VA to do your marketing for free as an exchange for the business you brought them.

Automating the Optimal Marketing Strategy

The next step in developing an Optimal Marketing Strategy is automation. In order to automate your marketing, you need to acquire the right team, technology, and outsourcing solutions available to consistently execute on the optimal marketing strategy.

The good part is that once you find your OMS, automating it is simple. In other words, if you know the button to push to get the customers you need, then it is just a matter of getting your team, technology, or outsourcing solution to push the button for you.

The 3 Day Entrepreneur is constantly looking for systems that will allow them to fully automate their marketing. Here are few examples of ways the 3 Day Entrepreneur automates their optimal marketing strategy, which boosts their ROI substantially:

1. **Design an Emotionally Compelling Website add SEO/ PPC—** Having a website that works as an online brochure is helpful. However, the 3 Day Entrepreneur puts the resources and effort in producing an emotionally compelling website that will motivate visitors to take action, through either a purchase, a call, or an email.

   This also means having an effective search engine optimization (SEO) program, or pay-per-click program working for you. You will want your website to come up on the first page of search engines for the major key words or phrases that your customers use to search for your product or service.

2. **Targeted Landing Pages—**Having a website is good, but the 3 Day Entrepreneur understands it's better to have multiple, targeted landing pages (a landing page is a 1 page website) designed to motivate visitors to take action. The call to action can be a sale, a call, or to capture more and more of your prospects emails. It mostly includes giving away something valuable for free (E-book, Tip sheet, newsletter, etc.) in exchange for your prospect's contact information.

3. **Email Marketing and Autoresponders—**Once you have acquired your prospect's contact information, you can begin to send out emails to your new database. You can set it up so that an email is automatically sent out every week, or every 2 weeks. This way you can stay in the customer's mind all year, and provide offers that your customers can take advantage of.

4. **Commissioned Sales People—**The 3 Day Entrepreneur understands the value in contracting commissioned sales people. We know that once you have identified the Optimal Marketing Strategy, the next step is to increase the amount of work you do in finding leads. The answer is the commissioned sales person.

   The 3 Day Entrepreneur uses commissioned sales people to do the day-to-day work of finding new leads, and following up with leads, and getting in front of decision makers they can sell to. Also, because commissioned sales people only wear one hat, they are experts at what they do, and produce consistent results.

The best sales people are those that provide solutions for their clients. They are able to teach their clients, challenge their clients, tailor their message to their clients, and take control of a sale in order to lead it to where it needs to go.

5. **Virtual Appointment Setters/ Telemarketers**—In order to cut the grunt work necessary in finding new customer leads, the 3 Day Entrepreneur hires appointment setters for the sole purpose of turning cold leads into warm leads. This frees up the sales people to focus on what they do best, which is identifying the decision makers and selling to them. The best part is that the appointment-setting person can work from a remote location, which gives the 3 Day Entrepreneur more opportunity to find great talent from around the nation, or even the world.

6. **High Value Referral Sources**—High value referral sources (other business people that serve your target market but don't compete against you), are one of the greatest sources of leads for the 3 Day Entrepreneur. Since these referral sources have direct access to the type of customers the 3 Day Entrepreneur needs, we should spend lots of time, effort, and resources identifying the ideal referral partners to do business with. Once we have established a network of 10–20 qualified referral sources, then nothing can stop the leads from coming in. These relationships continue for long time, as long as the referral partner sees value in the relationship.

7. **Affiliates**—Affiliates are just regular people that are highly motivated to tell their circle of friends and associates about your products and services. They are motivated because you give them a percentage of the sales they make. For a piece of the pie, they will pre-sell customers and make your life easier. Creating a huge affiliate force is a great way to have your own sales force without spending a dime upfront.

8. **Video**—YouTube is the second largest search engine next to Google. Not to mention the other hundreds of video sites on the web that people regularly go to. If you post an emotionally compelling sales video and people can find it, you will have a substantial amount of customers waiting at your door. You can also send it out to your email list, your contacts, etc.

9. **Advertisements**—Whether in print or online, ads are as effective now as ever. Find a great copywriter to write multiple ads for you and test the one that works best. The best part is, once you find an ad that works, it will bring you customers for many years to come.

10. **Direct Mail**—Just like advertisements, if you can create direct mail pieces that work, you can mail them out every few months and continue to get new customers coming to your business, year after year. Find a great copywriter and test different mail pieces to a small group. Once you find the most successful direct mail pieces, send it to a larger group.

For a complete list of different ways to automate your marketing go to www.the3dayentrepreneur.com/resources.

Exercise

1. Pick 3–4 automated marketing systems from the previous list that you believe can work for your business.

2. Implement these automated marketing systems, consistently, for the next 30 days.

3. Track your results.

4. At the end of 30 days, evaluate your results. Keep what worked, replace what did not work.

Conclusion

The 3 Day Entrepreneur does not do marketing just to get a customer. Rather, we are interested in finding the Optimal Marketing Strategy that can bring in customers for life. We can usually find the OMS by focusing on what successful competitors do, what has worked in the past, and what always works. The 3 Day Entrepreneur also works to automate their OMS so that they can provide their business with all the customers they need, while using the least amount of time, effort and resources to do it.

CHAPTER 13

The Optimal Sales Strategy

"Everyone lives by selling something."
Robert Louis Stevenson

There is no better area for the 3 Day Entrepreneur to create massive value than in the area of selling.

We define selling as the ability to increase the value of a product or service in the mind of a customer, so that they would gladly pay the prices we ask. Because of this, the 3 Day Entrepreneur focuses on specific areas that will not only produce more sales, but also magnifies the amount of money that can be made from each sale. As you continue to improve the sales system, it results in creating a selling process that consistently produces high value sales. This is also known as The Optimal Sales Strategy (OSS).

The First Step of the OSS— Knowing Your Ideal Customer

The first and most essential element of the 3 Day Entrepreneur Optimal Sales Strategy involves creating a system for identifying your Ideal Customer. The Ideal Customer is the person best positioned to buy your product and services because they have a need for it, and they have the means to pay the prices you ask.

The better you can get to know your ideal customer (also known as profiling your customer), the easier it is to find them and sell to them.

It's very similar to wildlife watching. For example, suppose you were looking for buffalo. Where would you go? Would you go to the cities of New York City? Probably not. You would probably go to the plains of Africa. Once you make it to Africa, do you go to the local hotel? Or do you go out in the wild? And once out in the wild, do you know what their grazing patterns are? Do you know their favorite watering hole, their mating rituals, their sleeping habits, or their favorite meal?

The idea is that the more you know about your ideal customer, the better chance you will have for not only finding them, but also finding hundreds more of them that follow similar patterns.

The 3 Day Entrepreneur understands that the more clear the lifestyle patterns of their ideal customers become, the easier and quicker it will be to find them. And not only find them, but since you know them so well, you can easily motivate them to buy the products and services that they are probably already searching for.

Profiling Your Ideal Customer

The 3 Day Entrepreneur tries to know their prospects and customers better than they know themselves. Here is a list of things you should understand about your ideal customers:

1. Yearly income.
2. Gender.
3. Family status (single, married, parents, etc.)
4. Culture (Gen X, Gen Y, Baby boomer, etc.)
5. Ethnicity (white, African American, Hispanic, etc.)
6. Where they live.
7. Where they work.
8. What they read.
9. What media they use.
10. Where they get their information.
11. Where they spend most of their time.
12. Their favorite past times and hobbies.
13. What they spend most of their time doing.
14. Biggest needs and desires.
15. Biggest fears and concerns.
16. Biggest pleasures.
17. Buying criteria and habits.
18. How they want to be introduced to a new product or service.
19. Typical financial status (poor, middle-class, affluent, etc.).
20. How they feel about your product or service.

For a complete list of questions to ask to thoroughly profile your ideal customer, go to www.the3dayentrepreneur.com/resources.

On the other hand, consider the typical entrepreneur that only knows a few pieces of information about their prospect. How do you think the prospect will respond if the entrepreneur misses the prospect's needs entirely? Or, what if the entrepreneur offers their product or service without first knowing the prospect's most important buying criteria? The chances for a sale begin to dwindle dramatically.

By knowing vast amounts of information about your prospects, the 3 Day Entrepreneur is better able to start a buying conversation with your ideal customer. You'll be able to convey your message in such a way that the customer feels that you're not selling, but helping them buy. And you do this by continuing the conversation that is already going on in the prospect's head. Knowing so much about a prospect allows the 3 Day Entrepreneur to greatly influence the customer's buying decisions, which generally results in a sale.

Qualifying Prospects

Another area where you can get great leverage is in the area of qualifying prospects.

To the 3 Day Entrepreneur, qualifying means putting their prospects through a highly strict filter, so that it results in only spending their time with the prospects that are best able to buy.

You see, not all customers are created equal, and their value varies greatly. This makes it a priority to spend your time with the most valuable prospects. These are the prospects that have the following characteristics:

1. They have a strong need and desire for the product or service;

2. They have the means to pay the prices asked; and

3. They are better able to purchase over and over, over a long period of time (also known as, the customer's long-term value).

Here are some typical ways the 3 Day Entrepreneur qualifies their prospects:

- Have a prepared script with questions to ask the prospect that will help get a better understanding of the value of the prospect.

- Have a phone interview with prospects to determine if they are an ideal customer.

- Have the prospect fill out a form online, when they inquire about your products or services. This helps in filtering out the serious from the not so serious prospects. It also provides information that can be later used for evaluating the prospect's other needs for future sales.

- Have prospects send in a proposal in order to try to win the company's business (puts you in the authoritative role.)

- Post prices on the marketing and sales materials in order to scare away prospects not willing to pay the prices asked.

The Sales Process

After you have has identified your ideal customer, you then need an effective sales process to move the prospect toward a decision to buy.

The sales process is designed to lead a prospect to realize that their obvious and best choice is to buy the product or service that you are offering them. The more skillful and effective the sales process, the quicker and smoother the sale goes. This is why the 3 Day Entrepreneur continually improves their sales process, until they can consistently produce a successful sale, over and over again. An effective sales process that consistently takes prospects from appointment to closing the sale is the foundation of the Optimal Sales Strategy.

Here are the most essential elements to use in your sales process to consistently get sales:

1. **Build Rapport**—Build an emotional connection with the prospect in order to quickly gain their respect and trust.

2. **Help them Feel the Pain of the Problem**—Help the prospect feel the pain of the problem they came to see you for. This can be done by asking questions that describe the consequences of the problem for the customer, such as "What kind of challenges is this problem creating for you?"

3. **Identify their Buying Criteria**—Identify the 3 most important buying criteria the prospect uses in making buying decisions, and why. This can also be done with a simple question like, "What are the most important qualities you are looking for in this kind of product?"

4. **Create Massive Value**—Create value in the mind of the prospect by using skillful questions, stories, metaphors, statistics, etc. The goal is to help the prospect feel the consequences of not taking action, as well as the benefits and rewards for using your solution.

5. **Demonstrate Capability**—Show how your solution meets every one of the important buying criteria of your prospect. The important thing is to focus only on their most important buying criteria. Otherwise your prospect will feel like you are selling something they don't want or need.

6. **Reduce the Risk**—Help reduce the risks of the buying decision in the mind of your customer (use testimonials, endorsements, money back guarantees, etc.).

7. **Ask for the Sale**—Call your prospect to make a decision to use your solution. Again, a simple question can close the sale, such as, "So, when would you like to get started?"

8. **Help Reinforce the Decision**—Help reinforce their buying decision by helping them see more of the future benefits and rewards of their decision. You can do this with a simple question such as, "How do you think you will most benefit from this solution?"

The Gateway Sale

The 3 Day Entrepreneur understands that once a prospect is able to overcome all the risks in buying, and they emotionally step into a buying relationship with the sales person, then every sale afterward will come much easier.

Because of this, we should begin a relationship with a customer through the sale of a low-priced but valuable item. The price does not matter, because what is most important is the emotional step the prospect has taken to begin a relationship with the salesperson. Similar to dating, once you have coffee with a person and have a good time, it is much easier to get them to go out to dinner. This is known as a Gateway Sale.

Often times, if the 3 Day Entrepreneur does not make the big sale, they will default to their gateway offer in order to help the prospect take the next step. The gateway offer can also be used to begin a relationship with a reluctant buyer, because the big sale may be too risky for them.

Here are typical gateway offers to help your prospect take the next step in the buying relationship:

- Sell them a smaller version of the product or provide a smaller service package, instead of the big product or service.
- For informational products, sell a book or E-book, in lieu of a full-service coaching program.
- Sell the design, instead of the full construction project.
- Offer an initial consulting evaluation, instead of the full-service consulting engagement.

 ·• Offer an online market analysis, instead of the overall web marketing program.

The 3 Day Entrepreneur also makes sure that the gateway product or service costs them next to nothing to provide. By providing it inexpensively, and in a passive and automated way, it leverages them even more.

3 Sources for Quick Sales

Here are 3 sources that will give you the quickest and easiest sales to boost your cash flow, and build momentum in your business:

Source 1 — Previous customers

Your previous customers have a 50–80% chance of buying from you again. Now is the time to contact them to see if they are in need for more of your products or services.

Source 2 — Previous prospects (people who previously said no to your offer)

97% of consumers are not ready to buy right now, but they will buy at some point. It is time to go back and see if these previous prospects are now ready to purchase your products or services.

Source 3 — Current Customers

50% of customers will buy additional products and services if they are asked at the time they purchase. (Remember the McDonalds slogan, "Would you like to supersize that?") They will also buy from you again at other times, just because you made the suggestion. It's time to offer more products and services, by training ourselves and our salespeople to ask, and provide our customers with more options to buy.

Automating the Optimal Sales Strategy

Ultimately, the 3 Day Entrepreneur understands that once the Optimal Sales Strategy has been tested and developed, someone or something else can now reproduce the same results. This allows you the opportunity to greatly expand your efforts.

For example, once you have identified the best script to turn your leads into customers, you can hire a commissioned sales person to go out and produce the same results. This not only frees you or your sales team up, but it provides an opportunity to expand your business to as big of a capacity as you can handle.

Here are some of the tools the 3 Day Entrepreneur uses to automate their Optimal Sales Strategy.

The Core Story

The core story is an idea made famous by Chet Holmes, from his landmark book, *The Ultimate Sales Machine*. The core story is basically the company's main marketing and sales presentation, which takes a prospect through the entire buying process. Its emphasis is to emotionally tap into the deepest needs, fears, and desires of the prospect and to communicate all of the major benefits and rewards of making a purchase. It is so effective that it motivates even the most skeptical prospect into buying. The core story is also the main source for all of your other marketing and sales materials.

Similar to the Effective Sales Process, here are the main elements of an effective core story:

1. **Establish Rapport**—Emotionally connect with the prospect, and influence them to want to know more.

2. **Buying criteria**—Tap into their major buying criteria, further establishing rapport.

3. **Tap into their Major Problems**—Help them tap into the pain of their problem, and the major consequences they will face by not taking action to resolve their problems (use statistics, case studies, etc. in order to drive the point home.)

4. **Make a Promise**—Describe the different solutions that will resolve the prospect's problems, subtly emphasizing your company as the ideal solution.

5. **Show Proof**—Share testimonials, case studies, statistics, credentials, etc. to show your capability to fulfill on the promises you make.

6. **Push**—Call them to action to take the next step (call, email, visit, etc.).

For a template on how to write an effective core story, go to www.the3dayentrepreneur.com/resources.

Sales Scripts

The 3 Day Entrepreneur understands that a great sales script is like a goose that lays golden eggs. The sales script is designed to consistently get a sale whenever there is a qualified prospect to sit in front of. The words used, the flow of the script and the message conveyed are designed to have such an influential effect on the prospect, that it eventually leads them to seeing the product or service as the obvious choice.

The script is designed by using information you collect from the Ideal Customer Profile and the Core Story. It is designed to touch the prospects main pleasure and pain points. The script is then tested multiple times in the field, improving it after every use, until it can produce the best results over and over again.

Once the script can succeed at getting sales, 6 out of 10 times, it can be tested by other sales people in the field until it produces the same result for them as well.

Sales Presentations

A Sales Presentation is a smaller version of the core story, and it uses visual aids, pictures or videos to further influence a prospect to buy. Presentations are usually done through PowerPoint or Keynote, with the use of emotionally compelling slides to motivate the prospect to action. Use of special visual effects are also successfully used to influence the prospect.

The material for the Sales Presentation comes mainly from the Ideal Customer Profile and the Core Story, with emotionally compelling stock photo used to drive the main points home. Video is also used, again to further emotionally motivate the prospect to action.

The 3 Day Entrepreneur uses presentations either for one-on-one sales meetings with a prospect or in front of a group of potential buyers.

Sales Seminars

Seminars are the favored venue for making sales because of the obvious leverage that comes from having a large group of qualified people to sell to. It also provides great value because of the massive amount credibility attributed to the speaker. The 3 Day Entrepreneur understands that audiences automatically attribute expert status to speakers at seminars, and they use this to their benefit. Once the 3 Day Entrepreneur speaks, they are considered a specialist, resulting in increased trust, which inevitably leads to more sales.

The 3 Day Entrepreneur may further leverage themselves by using technology to conduct online selling webinars, or conference call seminars over the phone. By leveraging themselves in this way they are able to reach more and more people throughout the country and the world.

Sales Letters

Sales letters are on obvious tool of choice for the 3 Day Entrepreneur because of the massive reach an effective sales letter can have in the marketplace. Effective sales letters have historically generated billions of dollars in revenue for companies that use them. The benefit of sales letters is that they can be distributed through the mail, through the internet, television, or other media channels, giving the 3 Day Entrepreneur a great opportunity for massive sales.

The value of a sales letter also comes from its simplicity. It has all of the emotionally compelling elements of the core story, and it is aimed at the most qualified prospects. Best of all it can be reproduced on a massive scale. It can also be converted into other media such as a video sales letter or an advertisement over the radio.

Because the effectiveness of a sales letter depends on the quality of the writing, the 3 Day Entrepreneur invests in hiring the best writers (known as copywriters) to write multiple versions of their sales letter, and tests all of them in the marketplace. The winner of the test becomes the control letter to be sent out to the most qualified prospects. Later on, the sales letter can be further improved, creating even more sales for the business.

Sales Videos

Similar to sales letters, one of the ways the 3 Day Entrepreneur greatly leverages their sales results is through the use of a Sales Video. The Sales Video motivates prospects to buy, or take the next action step, through the use of emotionally compelling pictures, words, and sounds. It creates a full emotionally compelling experience that leads the prospect internally to making the obvious choice to buy.

A Sales video conveys the main selling points from the Core Story, but through a more engaging experience. Like the sales letter, the sales video can be distributed through multiple channels, throughout the internet, throughout the country and the world.

Commissioned Sales People

Last, a standard strategy used by the 3 Day Entrepreneur is to hire commissioned sales people to go out and use the Optimal Sales Strategy to win sales for the company.

Commissioned sales people generally only get paid when they make money for the company. This leverages the 3 Day Entrepreneur by providing them with the focused efforts of talented sales people, while costing very little money up front. And, you should pays high commissions to the sales people, because 80% of something is much greater than 100% of nothing.

Now, the 3 Day Entrepreneur doesn't hire just any sales people, but you hire the superstars that can create value for prospects and for the company. These sales people, normally known as "Challengers," are the most effective personality of sales people, regardless of the economic climate, as described by Matthew Dixon and Brent Adamson in their book, "The Challenger Sale."

Because of their personality, these type of sales people tend to be the most successful. Yet, they can be difficult to find, and even more difficult to manage. Although challenging, The 3 Day Entrepreneur looks forward to this challenge, because he or she understands that these types of sales people will stop at nothing to get the sale, persisting when 80% of other sales people give up. They create so much value that prospects and customers see them as valuable team members, and not just sales people.

Once you put together your A-level team of sales people, you can greatly expand your customer base, resulting in a massive growth in revenue, while using less time, effort, resources, and money.

Conclusion

The 3 Day Entrepreneur maximizes their sales potential by developing their Optimal Sales Strategy that consistently converts leads to sales. Then they take the OSS and through delegation, technology and efficient systems, multiply their results by automating the process. Ultimately, the 3 Day Entrepreneur will greatly multiply their incomes, because they spend the time developing and improving a sales system that brings massive revenue to their businesses.

CHAPTER 14

The Optimal Pricing Strategy

"Value is in the eye of the beholder."
Alan Weiss

Pricing is one of the best tools the 3 Day Entrepreneur can use to create massive value while leveraging their efforts.

The power in pricing comes from its flexibility. Pricing is basically the customer's willingness to pay whatever they think something is worth. In other words, pricing is based on the customer's perspective. The benefit of this is that if you can increase the value of your products or services in the mind of your customer, then they will be more willing to pay the prices that you ask.

It's like a seesaw. If the customer does not see much value in your product or service, then price will be an issue.

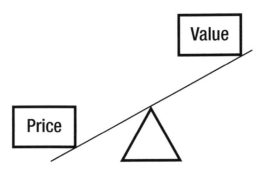

However, if you influence the customer to see more and more value in your products and services, then price becomes a non-issue. And if you create enough value, you can ask whatever price you want.

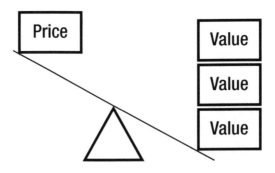

The idea is that as the value of the product or service increases in the mind of the customer, the price becomes less and less of an obstacle. And when value outpaces price, then you automatically have a sale.

The 3 Day Entrepreneur focuses on two main pricing areas to create more value for customers: the price amount and the price terms.

Influencing Price Amount and Price Terms

The Price Amount is simply the quantity that you are asking for in exchange for your products and services. In other words, "What" you will be paid. Price amounts are very flexible, and customers can be influenced to pay more through:

1. **Sales Skills**—Your ability to increase the value of your products and services in the mind of your customer, during your sales meetings and presentations greatly influences the prices you ask.

2. **Higher Value Customers**—The type of customer you are targeting, how much money they have to spend, and how much they value your products and services greatly influences how much you can charge.

3. **Bonuses**—The additional bonuses you offer with the product or service they are purchasing, temporarily boosts the value of your products and services in the eyes of your customer. This allows you to create promotions and charge higher prices people will pay for.

The Price Terms, on the other hand, are the way that you and your customers agree on "How" you will get paid. Here too we find a lot of room for flexibility and more ways to influence your client. Pricing Terms can also be influenced by:

1. **Sales Skills**—Like the Price Amount, this depends on your ability to increase the value of your products and services in the mind of your customer.

2. **The Customers You are Targeting**—Some customers will be more open to purchasing if the pricing terms fit their expectations.

3. **Customer Cash Flow**—If customers have tight budgets, flexible pricing terms give them the opportunity to purchase your product or service.

4. **Customer budgets**—Some customers have preset budgets and spending limits that flexible pricing terms would be a great fit for.

5. **Your Creativity and Negotiation Skills**—The more flexible you are, the more value you can create with your customer. This is because customers are willing to trade things that are important to them if their most important buying criteria is fulfilled. If the price amount is important to customers, they may be flexible on the price terms, or vice versa. Flexible pricing terms go a long way in influencing your customer to buy.

The Optimal Pricing Strategy

There are many opportunities to create great value in the area of pricing. Here is where we introduce the idea of the Optimal Pricing Strategy (OPS), which provides you with the highest possible profit, while using the least possible amount of your time and resources to produce it.

The Optimal Pricing Strategy creates a greater ROI by focusing on the following areas:

1. Targeting Higher Paying Customers

In the business to consumer (B2C) market, there are special individuals where price is rarely an issue. Even in a difficult economy these people have no problems spending a lot of money for what they consider valuable. These are the people that pay $400 for a haircut, or spend thousands of dollars for a coat stand.

At the same time, in the business to business (B2B) market, there are businesses that have substantial budgets already allocated for purchasing the products or services that you are selling. They are more than willing to spend their entire budget on what they perceive to be a high quality product or service.

If either of these types of customers sees enough value, they will be more than willing to spend more money, even if a competitor offered them a cheaper price.

The issue is that many entrepreneurs are so desperate for money that they will do business with just about any warm body that is willing to pay. Unfortunately, this kind of thinking generally attracts the wrong customers, especially those that care about price (or the cheapest price) more than anything else.

The 3 Day Entrepreneur, on the other hand, will spend a substantial amount of their time marketing and selling only to the customers that can afford the highest prices in the marketplace. They will also make a deliberate effort to qualify (filter out), deter and avoid any price customers. Higher paying customers mean more profit, and less time and effort invested; ultimately resulting in a higher return.

The 3 Day Entrepreneur also understands that there are many uber wealthy customers in the marketplace as well. These clients, normally known as Dream Clients, Anchor Clients, or Whales, are those individuals or companies that, if you land their business, will provide substantial business for years to come. Though these clients take time to acquire, the 3 Day Entrepreneur consistently pursues these clients, until he or she sells them. The 3 Day Entrepreneur understands that one of these clients alone can leverage them so dramatically that it will result in substantially higher profits, with minimal effort.

2. Charge the Highest Prices

There is always someone in every industry that charges the highest prices. They do this because they know that someone will pay for it. And, if they are still in business after a few years, it means that they have found a good source of ideal customers willing to pay these prices.

Another benefit of charging the highest prices is that customers tend to place a higher value for your products and services if they are more expensive. In other words, the higher the price you charge for your products and services, the more valuable people will consider it, and more importantly, the easier it is to sell at that price.

A third benefit of charging a high price is that by charging more, you will naturally attract the kind of customers who are used to paying those prices. Therefore, it makes attracting your ideal customer much easier. Also, the high price tends to filter out all the cheapskates who are not your ideal customers.

How to Raise Prices and Have Customers Thank You For It

Raising prices is one of the best ways to double your profits because all the extra money goes straight into your pocket. As a matter of fact, a 1–5% increase in price can result in a 10–40% increase in profits.

Yet, isn't our greatest fear that if we raise prices we will lose customers, or that our new customers will go somewhere else that's cheaper? Well, I want to show you a simple way to raise prices that customers will thank you for.

The Bonus

Price is determined by the amount of value that your customers see in your product or service. Simply, if they see lots of value they will be willing to pay a higher price.

What if you could quickly boost the value in your customer's eyes, enough so that they will be willing to pay more for it? That's where the bonus comes in.

A bonus is something that you add to your product or service that is highly valuable in the customer's eyes, but is very inexpensive for you to provide.

Here are some ideas of bonuses that you can provide that are inexpensive for you, yet valuable for your customer:

1. **Special free gift**—Find a vendor to give you product for free or sell it to you at cost (Remember, one man's trash is another man's treasure). Then give it to your customer with their purchase as a "Free Gift" for purchasing.

2. **Add a service to a product**—Provide services with your products that only costs you time, but that the customer values greatly. Free consultation, support, and access to resources are all examples of services you can add to your product to boost its value.

3. **Add a product to a service**—Find a product that your customer needs with your service. Partner with a vendor to provide it. Provide it as an add-on to their purchase and it greatly increases the product's value.

4. **Free advice/free report**—A report or video on a subject your customer likes can boost value. Meanwhile it will cost you a few hours to put it together.

5. **Bundle items together**—Put products or services together, that your customer values, but that cost you close to nothing to provide.

6. **Convenience**—Provide more convenience for your customers (open earlier, free shipping, etc.) without utilizing a lot of time or money.

7. **Special packaging**—Providing the product or service in a package that your customers value greatly also increases its value. Adding a lot of bells and whistles may allow you to add an extra zero to the price tag that the customer will gladly pay (I.e.: Tiffany's little blue box).

8. **Special arrangement**—Provide the product or service in a more beneficial format for the customer (I.e.: packaged deals versus a la carte purchases).

9. **Payment options**—provide payment options that make it easier for your customers to pay, like a monthly payment versus lump sum.

10. **Value pricing**—Add more bonuses for customers that will pay more, less for those who will not.

Once you find the bonus that works and provide it as an incentive for raising prices, you will be able to raise prices and your customers will be so glad you did.

3. Modify Pricing Terms

Pricing terms can be modified so that it results in greater revenue over the long term, and more convenience for the customer.

As we mentioned before, one of the biggest benefits of pricing is that it is highly flexible. If you can convince a prospect of the massive value a product or service has in solving their problem, you can substantially increase the price, and the customer will gladly pay it. However, if the customer is temporarily limited in their cash flow, you can modify the terms to your benefit and for the convenience of the customer.

For example, you can change the payment terms from a lump sum payment to monthly installments. Or, you change the pricing terms from being paid upon receipt, to giving terms for 30, 60 or 90 days. Another option would be that instead of full upfront payment, you can be paid a deposit up front, and the rest upon completion, with a fee paid for the use of this option.

Consider this example: if I offer my client a 6 month consulting package for a lump sum of $10,000, they may be more willing to pay it if I bill them $2000 per month over a 6 month period. This is appealing to the client because they do not have to come up with the lump sum payment, and I am happy because now I am getting paid $12,000 instead of $10,000. Also, I have created a recurring revenue stream for the next 6 months.

4. Provide Unique Pricing Terms

Another opportunity comes from the ability to negotiate a fee for the use of unique pricing terms. For example, if the standard in my industry is to get a lump sum payment for a product or service, I can allow the client to pay in monthly installments for a long period, and charge them a monthly fee for this privilege. In other words, you create a financing arrangement with the client, and in the end, you make more money than you would normally sell it for.

Another way to increase the return on investment in this type of financing arrangement is to charge a hefty late fee. The benefits are that not only does it motivate some customers to pay on time, you also benefit from those that don't.

5. Use Pricing Options

The 3 Day Entrepreneur converts prospects into customers by helping the prospect change their mindset from "If" they will hire you, to "How" they will work with you.

This is accomplished by using pricing options. Pricing options are simply providing two or three pricing options for customers, instead of one. This shifts the potential customer's focus to choosing the best option, rather than if they will work with you at all.

A big benefit of using pricing options is that you are able to get both the amount and terms you are looking for more often. For example, if I am selling my consulting services, instead of providing just one option and price, I can provide the prospect with three:

6 Month Consulting Package
Option 1: $6000—Bare bones, basic service
Option 2: $10,000—Deluxe, more advanced valuable services included.
Option 3: $25,000—All the bells and whistles, and more.

The 3 Day Entrepreneur positions their best priced package as the middle option. This is because statistically, most customers choose the middle option. Their reasoning is that they need more than the basic package, but they may not be able to justify spending for all of the bells and whistles, so they choose the middle option. Therefore, by using pricing options, not only does the 3 Day Entrepreneur get the price that he or she wants, but all of the terms he or she desires as well.

7 Ways to Increase the Amount Customers Spend When They Purchase

You have many methods available to you to influence the price and terms of your products and services to motivate customers to buy more:

1. Provide a Menu of Options

Provide a menu of different options to serve different types of customers. Restaurants are a good example of this. They have the "Early Bird Special" for the more price conscious customers; and a "Chef's Special" for the customers willing to spend more. The benefit is that it expands your customer base. Just make sure the price customers are taken care of in a passive and inexpensive way.

2. Provide Different Versions of your Product or Service

Provide different versions of your product or service to serve different customer needs. For example a package delivery company can provide services for consumers or businesses, or for different needs (2 Day delivery or Next Day delivery.) Because these services are valued differently, you can charge substantially more for more valuable options.

3. Provide Payment options

Provide different payment options for different customers. By providing different payment options for different customers you greatly expand your customer base. Offer price customers a monthly financing option. Offer value customers a full-pay option with a discount or bonus.

4. Provide Long-term Customer Loyalty Programs

By setting up long-term contracts with customers, it gives you greater flexibility in influencing price, because you will be making more money. By being paid more over a long period you are more able to provide discounts to customers, motivating them to buy. These options include: purchase contracts, monthly memberships, retainer/fixed pricing options, etc.

5. Test New Products or Services at a Discount

Test a new product or service line by giving customers a discounted rate for being part of the test market group. The customer is happy to receive the product or service at a discount; you get a guaranteed purchase for new products and services.

6. Bundle Services and Products.

By combining products and services, they will have a higher perceived value and you can charge more.

7. Provide Guarantees

Remove the risk and it will lead to increased value to the customer. For example, you can provide a 12 month money back guarantee, or a free 2 year maintenance plan.

Conclusion

The 3 Day Entrepreneur understands that pricing provides a great opportunity to create massive value while reducing time and money. This is because price is greatly determined by customer perception. This provides you with the flexibility to increase the value of a product or service in the mind of the customer, and then increase the prices customers are willing to pay. Also, by influencing the terms in how customers pay, it provides more opportunities to increase revenue from customers, while providing more convenience to them. The greatest benefit that pricing provides is that it gives you the freedom to choose what to charge, instead of being a slave to what the marketplace dictates they have to charge.

CHAPTER
15

Increasing Customer ROI

> "A customer is like a Swiss Army Knife; they provide multiple levels of value if you know how to open them up just right."
>
> **Will Peña**

Another area where the 3 Day Entrepreneur is able to create massive value is through increasing the amount of money made per customer. As you've probably heard, it is 8 times harder and more expensive to get a new customer than to continue selling to a current one. Therefore, if you can make more money per customer, not only does it save you a great deal of time, effort and resources, but it brings you a killer ROI as well.

So how do you get your customers to give you more money?

Targeting the Right Customers

In previous chapters, we discussed that if you target the right customers, they will pay the prices that you ask, no matter how high. Remember, there are customers in the marketplace that do not have a problem spending thousands of dollars on a purse or even an umbrella stand. And if they find value in your services or products, they will spend that money on you.

But these types of customers purposely segregate themselves from the rest of society. Not that they are reclusive, but they choose to hang around their own kind. What I am saying is that you will have to make a deliberate effort to target the right neighborhoods, associations, country clubs, social circles, and businesses to find these individuals. However, once you find them and they begin to buy from you, they will continue to buy from you for a very long time, as well as tell their wealthy friends about you, too.

Exercise

1. Put together a profile of the highest paying customers in your industry.

2. Make a list of all the different places where groups of them can be found. (I.e.: Consumers—neighborhoods, associations, country clubs; Business—chambers of commerce, business associations, etc.)

3. Find a reputable direct mail company and send out a direct mail campaign to these individuals (Business or consumer).

4. Track your results, and improve on what worked, while discarding what did not.

Qualifying Customers

Now, just because you target the right type of customers it doesn't mean that there won't be a few rotten apples in the bunch. And, by rotten apples I mean "price" customers. "Price" customers are those special people that do not value what you sell, or your expertise. What is most important to them is getting the cheapest deal they can for what you offer. To them, the prize is in the price, and if they can get away with getting you to pay them to be your customer, they will.

Now these people aren't all bad, and you may have a business that sells primarily to this type of client (think McDonalds, and Wal-Mart.) However, if you really want to multiply your returns, you will need to go after the "value" customers. Value customers are those customers that truly find value in your solution, your expertise, and advice regardless of the price.

But how will you be able to tell the good customers from the bad ones? How can you tell the "Price" customers from the "Value" customers?

The 3 Day Entrepreneur sets up a system to qualify their customers, and filter out all price clients. Here are few ways that help them successfully filter out the wrong customers:

1. Set up phone interviews that ask qualifying questions, before meeting with potential customers.

2. Put your prices on your website or brochure, which tends to scare away price customers.

3. Charge an upfront set-up fee, or processing fee before doing business with anyone.

For a complete list of different ways to qualify potential customers, go to www.the3dayentrepreneur.com/resources.

By successfully qualifying your clients, you save the time, effort, resources and money going after people that are not interested, not qualified, and no fun. And it results in attracting more of the ideal high value clients into your business.

Point of Sale Opportunities

Statistically 50% of people will say yes if you were to sell them additional products and services at the point of sale. Certain names automatically come to mind when we think of this tactic. Names like McDonalds ("Would you like to supersize that?"), Panda Express ("Would you like egg rolls with that?"), Amazon ("Customers that bought that item also purchased these…"), and more.

Psychologically, customers are at the greatest emotional state for purchasing during the point of sale, because by purchasing they have already made a decision that you are trustworthy and that what you offer is valuable. This feeling will naturally extend to considering other offers that you give them, especially when they are at the peak of this emotional state during the point of sale.

By getting your customers to buy more at the point of sale, you'll not only make more money per customer, but it also saves you precious time and money trying to promote to them later. As the saying goes, "You need to strike the iron while it's hot."

Exercise

1. Make a list of other products and services you can offer customers at the point of sale of your main product or service.

2. Come up with a simple one-line script or phrase that will motivate your customer to buy at the point of sale. (I.e.: Do you want to Supersize that?)

3. Test it out on new customers that buy your main product or service.

Upselling and Cross-Selling

Consistent upselling and cross-selling is another tactic the 3 Day Entrepreneur uses to make more money per customer. Upselling is defined as offering the customer additional products and services that cost a lot more than the original product or service they purchased. Cross-selling, on the other hand, refers to selling customers additional services that are a good fit for them, but are usually the same price or less.

Now, why would your customer buy additional products and services from you? The biggest reasons are:

1. They trust you;

2. They've tried the previous product and service and are satisfied;

3. They are your biggest fans; and

4. They continuously refer other customers to you.

Because of all of this, the 3 Day Entrepreneur focuses 80% of his or her marketing efforts on marketing and selling to their current customers.

Also, by upselling and cross-selling more expensive or complementary products and services to your customers, it not only generates more revenue, but it also increases your customer's loyalty to your organization. Customers generally view upselling and cross-selling in a positive way. This is because they see it as you taking a genuine interest in their welfare. With upselling especially, the more they pay, the stronger their loyalty to your company becomes. It's like going from a dating relationship, to being engaged, and then getting the highest priced item (I.e.: getting married). The bigger the stakes, the greater the loyalty.

Last, the 3 Day Entrepreneur is always looking for the next product or service (or more expensive product or service) to sell to their existing client base. If they cannot create it, they partner with another company that can provide it for them, for a share of the profits. This is yet another example of how you can use even less time, effort, resources, and money, but make a whole lot more money per customer.

Customer Long-term Value

Increasing customer long-term value is another technique that The 3 Day Entrepreneur is constantly focused on. Long-term value is defined as the amount of money the customer will spend with your business over the life of their relationship with you.

For example, let's look at the long term value of a consulting client. Now, the average life of a consulting client is a 12 month period. They spend on average about $1000 a month. When you combine these numbers, you come up with a long term value of $12,000 ($1000 X 12 or $12,000.)

On the other hand, a CPA has customers whose average life is about 10 years. If these customers spend an average of $2000 per year, their long term value is $20,000 (10 X $2000 = $20,000).

Long term value is important to the 3 Day Entrepreneur because we know that the longer the relationship with the customer, the more revenue we can make per customer. Because of this, we constantly look for ways to build loyalty with our customers so that we can make many more offers to them.

The 3 Day Entrepreneur also understands that customers bring many other levels of value, besides being able to make one purchase. Here are some additional levels of value customers bring to a business:

1. They buy complementary products, services and accessories (cross-sales.)

2. The buy higher value products and services (upsells.)

3. They buy different types of products and services year after year.

4. They buys products and services for others like family, friends, associates, customers, partners, etc.

5. They refer friends and family who begin purchasing products and services.

6. They provide valuable customer feedback that helps increase the value of the business.

Since customers bring so much value, the 3 Day Entrepreneur is always looking for opportunities to make more connections with them, and eventually get them to buy more. Whether through a phone call, an email, a birthday or anniversary card, or a special customer appreciation event, they use these opportunities to connect with the customer, and eventually persuade the customer to purchase more and more.

For example, let's say a customer spends $300 once with your company. Through additional efforts on your part, the customer ends up buying 3 times a year for the next 5 years. Now, the long term value of the client is boosted from $300 to $4500.

What would make your customer want to buy more often from your business? Most likely, they have a recurring need. Or, you're able to show them needs that they did not know they had. Either way, it creates an opportunity to sell them additional products and services, and motivate them to keep coming back to buy for years to come.

Tips to Re-engage with Customers for Additional Sales

Here is a list of ways to create more opportunities to reconnect with your customers to get more sales, and increase their long-term value:

1. **Specials/Discounts**—Send them irresistible offers that will motivate them to come back and purchase.

2. **Special Events**—Provide a special event (I.e.: customer appreciation, etc.) and invite your customers. At the event use the opportunity to reconnect with customers or provide an offer.

3. **Special Calls**—Give them a special call just to say "thank you." Later, send them an offer as a courtesy, because you "value them so much."

4. **Special Visits**—Take your highest value customers out to dinner, golfing, etc., and use the opportunity to create more business opportunities.

5. **Special Occasions**—Connect with them for their birthday, anniversary, holiday, etc. and use the opportunity to give them more offers.

6. **Survey, Review, or Feedback**—Invite your customers to come give you feedback, and use the opportunity to provide them offers for valuable purchases.

7. **Newsletter with Redeemable Offers**—Provide a weekly or bi-weekly newsletter with valuable information and occasional irresistible offers.

8. **Contest, prize drawing**—Set up an exciting contest and invite all your customers to join. Give them an irresistible offer as a reward for joining.

9. **Free Education**—Provide your customer with a free workshop or seminar that provides them with valuable information. Use the opportunity to connect at a deeper level, and send them an offer as a courtesy for coming.

10. **Charitable Event / Donation**—Have a charitable event, and encourage your customers to come by to drop off donation. Use the opportunity to connect with your customer and give them an irresistible offer.

For a complete list of ways to re-engage with your customers for additional sales go to www.the3dayentrepreneur.com/resources.

Winning Back Lost Customers

The 3 Day Entrepreneur knows that it is easier and less expensive to get a lost customer back than it is to get a brand new one. This is why he or she invests time and energy to not only preventing losing customers, but also trying to win old customers back. Lost customers are approached sensitively but with the deliberate intent to win them back, and getting them to start purchasing with the company again.

Here are few ideas the 3 Day Entrepreneur uses to win back old customers:

1. Contact the lost customer, apologize for any inconvenience and offer a bonus or discount for returning.

2. Send an email, text, or phone call to ask the lost customer for feedback, and provide them a bonus or discount as a reward for their help.

3. Send the lost customer a bonus or discount, just to thank them for their loyal patronage with the company.

4. Provide the lost customer a referral to a competitor, and get a fee from the competitor for the referral.

The ideal bonus or discount you provide a lost customer is usually toward a purchase at your business because it will help them to engage emotionally with your business once again. Once they remember the great experience they had with your company upon their return, their loyalty to your company will be stronger than ever, creating a paying customer for life.

Exercise

1. Make a list of all the previous customers you have served at your business.

2. Put together an irresistible offer as a gift to thank them for being a customer of your business.

3. Deliver it to them via email, direct mail, or phone.

4. Contact them a call to make sure they received it, and use the opportunity to re-engage your customer.

Conclusion

The 3 Day Entrepreneur is always looking for ways to expand the amount of revenue he or she can get per customer. They do this by targeting higher paying customers, cross-sells, upsells, and increasing the long term value of the customer. We also tap into our previous customer base, knowing that our previous customers can easily be made loyal again. The 3 Day Entrepreneur understands that a critical mass of qualified customers, when used to their full potential, can produce a massive amount of value and substantial profits for years to come.

CHAPTER
16

Maximizing
Your Team

"The strength of the team is each
individual member. The strength of
each member is the team."
Phil Jackson

The 3 Day Entrepreneur knows that if they want to expand the amount of value they create, they need the help of a powerful and capable team. In order to get their power team to create the most value, the 3 Day Entrepreneur focuses on four main areas:

1. The team members' capability.
2. The team members' talents.
3. The team members' energy.
4. The team member's integrity.

Capability

When we speak of capability, we mean the team member's mental, emotional, and physical ability to take on a substantial amount of work, and get the job done. For instance, if you have a person who is only able to do one task at a time, then your "leveraging ability" is going to be minimal. But the 3 Day Entrepreneur looks for a team of people with the capability to take on, not just one, but thousands of tasks. We understand that though all people are created equal, they have very different capabilities.

For example, some people can only do one task. Another person can take on multiple groups of tasks. A third person can manage or oversee a group of people who do different tasks. Finally, you have those individuals who are great at leading and motivating the leaders who lead others.

What does this all mean for the 3 Day Entrepreneur? This means that you ultimately have to prioritize all of your relationships. Of course you care about everyone in your business, but you must focus the majority of your attention on training and developing the individuals in the organization who have the most capability. In other words, you should spend most of your time with the people who are the leaders, who lead leaders, and who have the most ability to succeed at the most valuable parts of the business.

Talent

The 3 Day Entrepreneur also knows that in order to leverage a team effectively, they need to tap into their team's natural talents. You understand that people have natural talent and skill that they bring with them into the business. Whether through life experience, or their natural born abilities, they are excellent at some skill, and they love doing it. When people are excellent at what they do, and love doing it, they tend to do extremely well, and create substantial value for the business.

Therefore, you should leverage your team by first identifying people's talents and abilities, and then give them the opportunity to use those talents in the business. By using people's talents, you help people feel more motivated and invested in the success of the business.

When you hire someone, you should ideally make an effort to find out what all of their new team member's talents. And, not just in regards to the business itself, but in everything. Then you can position these team members in areas where they can use their talents to their fullest potential.

Here are a few ways to use a team member's talents for maximum benefit to the team member as well as the company:

1. **People who are good with people**—Some people are naturally great with people. So of course you don't want to put them in the back office dealing with paper work. Put them in front with your customers to create a great customer experience.

2. **Detailed Oriented People**—People with excellent organization skills may not be the best with customers, but they are excellent with managing and organizing the details of the business. Put them in the back office and give them the detailed tasks that help your business run at the level it needs to.

3. **Technically Oriented people**—Every organization has those few individuals that have a natural affinity toward technology and fixing things. These individuals feel at home understanding the ins and outs of the technology in your office. They are also constantly on top of the new technology that comes out, as soon as it comes out. Use these individuals to their fullest capacity by allowing them to oversee the maintenance of all of the technology in your business, as well as implementing new technology solutions.

4. **Artistic People**—Some people have been blessed by the Creator with the ability to create beautiful works of art that are visually stunning. What is best is that since people are emotionally influenced by their

visual senses, this person can be invaluable in your efforts to influence customers and vendors. Use them to their fullest capacity by allowing them the opportunity to express themselves in the office. It could be as simple as letting them redecorate the office, or as important as getting their input for the next marketing campaign.

5. **Diamonds in the Rough**—Sometimes you come across a special individual that is highly gifted in different areas, but who is raw and untrained. These are what I call "diamonds in the rough" in your business. Unfortunately, no one has taken the time to train to become a high powered leader. The 3 Day Entrepreneur is always on the lookout for these individuals to give them a chance to show what they are truly capable of.

From Will

 I remember I hired an intern in my organization to help me with some work I was doing. The first thing that I noticed when I met her was she was more mature than anyone that I had interviewed, even though she was only nineteen years old. She was the most mature person that I had ever met for her age, even more than some adults in their forties.

The more and more I got to know her, the more I noticed that her thinking was at a very high leadership level. Once I noticed it, I started training her by asking her leadership questions and getting her opinion on plans, customers, vendors, and testing her ability to handle difficult problems.

This did two things. One, it made her feel so incredibly important that she rose up into the leadership position that we were encouraging her to be in. And two, we now had an effective person in our organization who could deliver results.

Another big benefit was that because she was still young, she demanded very little in terms of salary. She just loved the value she received from being trained to become the woman she knew she could become.

Energy

Another aspect the 3 Day Entrepreneur looks for in a team member is energy. In other words, the amount of energy a team member can expend to accomplish his or her goals. You can have a person who is an incredible leader, but if their energy is not very high, it limits what they can do. This is because with more energy, comes more activity. So you should look for team members that have energy, and lots of it.

Another reason for this is that energy is contagious. So you need to look at the team members that have natural enthusiasm. Natural energy is the ability to get oneself to a peak emotional state, which allows one to keep on going. It is a powerful ability that is evident in only a select few. So the 3 Day Entrepreneur is constantly on the lookout for highly energetic people, so that they can use them to their full potential.

Integrity

The last characteristic the 3 Day Entrepreneur looks for is a team member's natural integrity. Strong integrity includes having a strong work ethic, high expectation of themselves, proactivity, their ability to create something out of nothing, and their natural ability to take charge of a task or project and to do the absolute best that they can. It also includes the habit of constantly evaluating oneself so that they can improve.

Now this kind of integrity and natural ability is obviously not found in everyone. But if you find it in your people, make sure you use it. Why? Because the 3 Day Entrepreneur is in the business of developing leaders that can lead other leaders. This ultimately results in creating a team that is self-motivated and self-sufficient, and who will be able to run the entire business on their own.

Team Management

Because time is limited, the 3 Day Entrepreneur makes sure that 90% of their time is spent with the highest quality people in the organization. If you're going to devote an hour to someone, devote that time with the person that can make the most out of it. And that person is generally part of your A-level leadership team.

What does the 3 Day Entrepreneur do with the rest of his or her time? Their remaining time is spent briefly encouraging other non-A level team members in the business. By only taking a minute or two to encourage other non-A level team members, it builds loyalty in the organization through maintaining healthy relationships. The 3 Day Entrepreneur constantly lets their people know how proud they are of them, or gives them feedback on the great things they are doing, as well as what they need to improve on.

But, again, give most of your time to the highest value leaders, which will produce the highest value results for the business, and can manage the rest of the organization for you.

Meetings

Any conversation about teams eventually leads to the topic of meetings. The common question is, "How do you manage a meeting in a way to get the most done?"

Now, are meetings important? Yes. However, do some meetings take up so much time that it renders them ineffective? The answer is absolutely. So how do you manage meetings to create the most value, use the most leverage and automation?

The 3 Day Entrepreneur's mindset about meetings is to make meetings as short as possible. According to Parkinson's Law, the shorter you make the meeting, the more it will force everyone to get things done in a more efficient way.

Use meetings for the purpose of making final decisions. Do this by preparing everyone beforehand for the meeting. This causes the meeting to flow toward the ultimate conclusion of making the most important decisions.

To prepare for a meeting, send everyone in the meeting the questions and topics of the meeting beforehand, so that they have more time to consider the information. This gives them the time to research, to reflect on the issues, and to come to general conclusions on the subject. So when they come to the meeting, they are ready with a list of ideas that have been thought through, which prepares them to make the best decisions.

Now do all meetings happen just for decision making? No. There is substantial value in having brainstorming meetings to come up with profitable ideas. But the key, again, is to keep things short. If you give the meeting two hours you will get what you need to get done in two hours. If you give it thirty minutes, you will get done what you need to get done in thirty minutes.

Conclusion

Teams are powerful vehicles for creating value and greatly leveraging your efforts. And in order to build the best team, you need to find the right team members in terms of their capability, talents, energy and integrity. Once you find your power team, you will spend 90% of your time and effort in training and developing them. As the team grows, they will take your business to greater levels of value, while freeing you up to do what you need to do.

CHAPTER
17

Leveraging
Finance

> "Just as a tiny acorn contains the power to grow into a mighty oak tree, each dollar bill has the power to grow into a mighty money tree."
> **Robert G Allen**

For the 3 Day Entrepreneur, the Finance area of the business provides a unique opportunity to create massive value. This is because we understand the great power money has in its ability to create even more money.

The 3 Day Entrepreneur has a special relationship with money. They see money as a tool that is used for the sole purpose of creating more value, which can then be exchanged for even more money. We can do this because we focus on 2 areas that, when used effectively, result in producing a massive amount of money in return. These areas are:

1. Spending Money Effectively
2. Leveraging Money Profitably

Spending Money Effectively

To start, the 3 Day Entrepreneur never uses the word "spending" in their vocabulary. It just doesn't exist. The only word that the 3 Day Entrepreneur uses to describe money going out of his or her organization is the word, "Invest."

This is because the only time that the 3 Day Entrepreneur lets money out of the business is when there is a definite opportunity to make money in return. The word "spending" suggests the idea of putting out money that you will never get back. The word "investing" on the other hand, describes putting money out temporarily that will bring many more dollars in return.

Because of this mindset, we're constantly searching for more ways to bring many more dollars back for every dollar we put out. Sometimes the return comes back as another type of value that can later be converted into more money. For example, if we pay for electricity to run the facility, we would instead invest the money in solar paneling to generate so much electricity it can take care of our own need, and sell the extra electricity back to the electric company for a profit.

The 3 Day Entrepreneur Investing Guidelines

Here are the four questions to ask yourself before making any spending ("investment") decisions:

1. **Is this something that the business needs or something that I want?**

   • For a business, needs are generally much more valuable than wants.

2. **Will this benefit us more now or will it benefit us more later?**

   • If you can benefit more by waiting, be patient and wait until later. Remember, money in hand is always more valuable than potential money later.

3. **What are other options that will provide what I need with less time, effort, resources and money?**

   - There are always better options; you just need to find them. Take a minute to consider other options, or ask advice from others.

4. **How can I increase my ROI for the money I am putting out?**

   - Remember every output of money must result in a greater return. Don't settle for just getting your investment back either, go for a higher and higher return every time.

The goal of these questions is so that every decision you make to spend (invest) money results in a better return. Therefore, if you can't answer all of these questions positively, don't put out the money. So, by following this guideline, the 3 Day Entrepreneur more guarantees that every dollar invested will bring many others back with them.

Expenses or Opportunities?

Most entrepreneurs think that paying expenses in the business is unavoidable. The 3 Day Entrepreneur, on the other hand, is always looking for ways to make every dollar that goes out generate a return. Here is a list of ideas they use to turn expenses into opportunities to make money:

1. **Race Monthly Bills** — If you can schedule your bills to be due on the same day, you can then deposit the money for monthly expenses in an interest bearing account or a liquid high yield account to earn interest on the money before it is paid out.

2. **Pay Expenses with Investment Income** — If you calculate the total amount of expenses for a quarter or a year, and invest this amount of money in a high yield investment or business, you can pay your

monthly bills on the monthly stream of investment income your investment produces.

3. **Cash Back Cards**—Use your cash back credit cards to pay all your monthly expenses and you will be able to receive cash back that will reduce your overall expenses.

4. **Install Your Own Utilities**—If you have the capital, install equipment that will provide your own utilities. If you generate extra, you can sell it to others for a profit (I.e.: Solar paneling produces electricity you can sell back to the electric company.)

5. **Resell Bill Paying Services**—If you find an inexpensive service that manages and pay all your expenses, you can resell these services to your competitors at a higher price, and keep the difference. Use the income from this to pay your own bills.

6. **Create a bill paying service**—If you design an efficient service in-house that helps manage all of your expense payments, you can rent this service out to competitors and use the income from this business to pay your own bills.

Saving vs Investing

Another concept the 3 Day Entrepreneur sees differently is the idea of "saving" money. Saving suggests the idea of money that is sitting somewhere, not doing much of anything. To the 3 Day Entrepreneur, every dollar is like a little laborer that works hard to bring home a whole lot more dollars. Locking that little worker in a vault, bank, or mattress will render the little worker useless. Gaining interest that hardly keeps up with inflation is also useless.

Rather, don't keep your money idle. Instead, put it to work in different ways that can generate more money. It could be lending it to someone for a much higher return, or it could be purchasing ownership in another business that brings a consistent stream of income.

Now, the 3 Day Entrepreneur understands the benefit of having reserves, but they invest those reserves so that instead of lying idle, they are generating even more money.

7 Ways to Leverage Your Reserves and Make Your Money Work for You

Here are a few ways the 3 Day Entrepreneur puts their reserves to work to make more money, instead of just sitting in a bank:

1. **Loans**—Lend money to other businesses or consumers for a fee or interest rate. Use their assets as collateral for the loan.

2. **Seed money**—Provide seed money to a business start-up in your industry that is similar to what you are currently doing, in exchange for an ownership stake, or a present share in the profits.

3. **Passive Investments**—Invest your cash reserves in investments with different ROI, based on their short term, or long term liquidity.

4. **Cash Cows**—Invest your cash into a "cash-cow" business that provides your business an additional, consistent stream of income.

5. **New Product or Service Lines**—Invest in building an additional product or service line in your business that brings additional income.

6. **Improvements**—Invest in improving your products and services so they can bring even more money to your business.

7. **Marketing**—Use your reserves to invest in effective marketing that will bring in even more money to your business.

Leveraging Money Profitably

To the 3 Day Entrepreneur, money is like energy. The one benefit about energy is that it can take on many forms and be converted from one form to the next. Money is similar in that it can be converted into many different forms of value, all of which can eventually lead to making even more money.

For example, you can take money and invest it in a business. The business works to make more money, and after a few years your initial investment results in making 5 to 10 times more money back. Or, you can convert money into an asset that appreciates over time (like real estate), to produce a lot more money when it is sold. Money can also be converted into valuable information (like publishing a book or an information product), that when sold can produce even more money. Lastly, money can be converted into a profitable system (like a passive business) that can produce more and more money for years to come.

Planting Money Trees

Money is like a seed that if planted correctly, can grow into a big tree that one day will feed you and your family for generations. Here is a list of ways the 3 Day Entrepreneur can plants money seeds so that they can grow into a very large money trees:

1. **Lending**—Lend money to someone else and receive interest back for letting them use the money.

2. **Buy Appreciating Assets**—Use money to buy an appreciating asset and sell it for a greater amount than what you originally used to purchase it.

3. **Expertise/ Consulting**—Use money to buy special knowledge or training that motivates others to hire you for your expertise, giving you a stream of income.

4. **Rentals**—Rent space with your money, and then divide the space so you can rent it out to others.

5. **Leasing Skilled Labor**—Hire a skilled employee with your money, then lease out their services to others who need them also.

6. **Buy Wholesale/Sell Retail**—Invest money to buy a product wholesale, and then resell it at a higher value.

7. **Specialized Equipment**—Invest money to buy specialized parts. Put them together to create a special machine that people will be willing to pay plenty of money to use or own. (I.e.: manufacturing equipment, etc.)

8. **Leasing Equipment**—Invest money to rent equipment, then lease it to many other people, and make multiple times your money in return.

9. **Repackaging/ Bundling**—Buy inexpensive products and services and repackage them in a bundle to sell them at a much higher price to others that value the combination.

10. **Auctions**—Buy products and then create an auction where people bid up the price so high that you make plenty of money at the end of the auction when the products are sold.

11. **Ecommerce/ Affiliate Services**—Invest money to advertise products or services you do not own. When people make a purchase, find another company that can fulfill it, and you receive a percentage or spread of the profits.

12. **Great Experiences**—Use money to create such a great experience for people that others will pay a lot of money to be part of it.

13. **Training and Development**—Invest in acquiring specialized knowledge that you can then re-teach to many others for a fee.

14. **Licensing**—Use money to make a valuable name, idea, book or manuscript, and then license it out to others for a hefty yearly fee.

15. **Investing in a Startup**—Use your money to invest in another person's business idea and their business efforts. Receive a percentage of the profits and ownership in the venture, which when sold will produce a hefty amount of more money coming to you.

Conclusion

In conclusion, the 3 Day Entrepreneur has such a resourceful relationship with money that it allows them to multiply their returns many times over. This is because the way they spend/ invest it, convert it, and leverage it, results in massive value being created. Then this value is converted easily into a great amount of more money. The end result is that the 3 Day Entrepreneur not only creates more time and freedom, but a substantial amount of wealth to boot.

CHAPTER
18

Optimizing Operations

"Efficiency is doing better what is already being done."
Peter Drucker

The final area the 3 Day Entrepreneur leverages, in order to create greater value, is in the day-to-day operations of the business.

We know that there are always opportunities to work in a more efficient manner. What motivates us to be more efficient is that if we can reduce the amount of time, effort, resources, and money used to run the day-to-day operations of the business, we will naturally create a higher ROI.

The Value of Systems

The 3 Day Entrepreneur is able to produce great results over and over again. This is because we rely on systems to make the business operations run effectively.

Systems are step-by-step instructions that can be followed by many people, and still produce the same result over and over again. Now, the 3 Day Entrepreneur relies on systems because they have 3 very important characteristics that help run the business effectively. These are:

1. **Systems are unemotional.**
2. **Systems are reliable.**
3. **Systems are reproducible.**

Systems are Unemotional

Why does it matter that systems are unemotional? Because nothing makes a business come to a grinding halt more than when the business owner is emotionally influenced by their circumstances. Systems, on the other hand, prevent this from happening because they force the business to continue to keep producing the same result, in spite of how the business owner feels or in spite of the circumstances.

In other words, systems change the business from being dependent on the character, personality, and emotional ups and downs of the business owner, and turn it into a machine that cranks out high value results, in spite of them.

Systems are Reliable

Another benefit of systems is that they create consistency. Consistency is the ability to produce the same or better results over a long period of time. In business, producing an increasing amount of value over a long period of time ultimately leads to long-term success. And, by knowing what to expect, it helps us build a business that produces massive value for years to come.

This is the main reason why, even though the success rate for entrepreneurial business startups are depressingly low, the success rate for franchises are extremely high (93% of franchises succeed according to statistics from the time this book was written). This is because franchises continue to rely on proven systems that consistently produce the returns they need in order to succeed.

Systems are Reproducible

The 3 Day Entrepreneur is interested in ways to create more value, while leveraging their time. This includes delegating the workload, so they can free themselves up to focus on the highest value tasks. But, how do you guarantee that someone else you delegate to will be able to create the high quality results that you do?

Again, we find the answer in the system. By documenting the step-by-step formula that is needed to create great results, another person will be able to follow those exact steps and create the same or an even better result.

The Benefits of Systems

Systems provide many very valuable benefits:

1. **Accuracy**—By giving your team a detailed system, instead of instructions from your head, you can more guarantee they will produce the result you want.

2. **Consistency**—As we mentioned previously, systems make sure that things are done the way you want them to, each and every time.

3. **Quality**—Customers look for specific and valuable benefits in the services and products they purchase. Systems guarantee that their expectations will be met, or exceeded, on a consistent basis.

4. **Recovery**—When mistakes are made, systems help the business recover quickly. This is because once a system is created for the problem, then the problem never returns, helping the business continually improve.

5. **Profitability**—Systems allow someone else to do what you do. This provides the opportunity to take your system and sell it to someone else. The system becomes an asset that can be sold, or licensed because of the value it creates for anyone who uses it.

How to Develop the Best Systems

There are no good or bad systems, only levels of effectiveness. As a 3 Day Entrepreneur, we focus on a few criteria in order to make systems effective. These are:

1. A convenient way to document systems.

2. A simple way to keep the systems user-friendly.

3. A practical way to test the systems to make sure they work.

Documenting Systems

Documenting means putting your system in some kind of vehicle that makes it easy for other people to get the information. Systems can be written, recorded as an audio, or put on video. The main purpose is to make it easy for others to follow directions.

Here are just a few examples of ways to document a system:

- Write a step-by-step user manual.
- Create a video of someone demonstrating the system.
- Create an audio that gives step-by-step directions on how to do something.
- Do a physical, hands-on demonstrations for your people.
- Put together educational, hands-on seminars and workshops to train a group.

The 3 Day Entrepreneur tries to combine the visual, audio and physical aspects when documenting a system, because these tend to be most effective. For instance, a video demonstrating a particular step-by-step process, with some hands-on exercises, generally delivers the best results.

Keep Systems User-Friendly

Obviously, we want the systems to be easy for anyone to use. In order to do this the system needs to be:

1. Not more than 15 steps long—10 steps preferably (a system with 63 steps will never be followed).

2. Written for a 9 year old or younger—The truth is that even the smartest people have difficulty with following instructions. The more understandable you make the system, the better chance that the instructions will be followed.

3. Accessible so that people can find it—If you have a great system that no one can find, it becomes useless. Make sure the system is either in a hard copy form that is located in a public place, or on a server, in a DVD collection, etc. The key is that people need to be able to find it, whenever they have a need.

Test to Make Sure It Works

Like team members, not all systems are created equal. A system that may work great for one person may be impossible to follow for someone else. The only way to know if others can use the system is to test it with others.

Try to get someone else in your business to follow the steps. If they understand the instructions, and are able to produce the same result, then you've hit the jackpot. But make sure you test it with more than one person so that it can truly be universal and reproduced by many other people.

To the 3 Day Entrepreneur, systems are the most crucial aspect of our toolbox. We should be determined to create systems for every aspect of the business. This is because the more work we are able to delegate, automate, and outsource, the more we can build greater value and leverage elsewhere. For the 3 Day Entrepreneur, systems rule our world.

Automation through Systemization

There are many types of systems that produce consistent results while creating a business that is not dependent on you:

1. Templates for every form in the business. (Customer forms, vendor forms, purchase forms, etc.)

2. Checklists for every system in the organization.

3. Step-by-step instructions for tasks or projects (video, audio or print).

4. Emergency procedures.

5. Preapproved vendor lists.

6. A Master Calendar.

7. Pricing lists.

8. Cash deposit procedures.

9. Accounts payable procedures.

10. Job roles and responsibilities

11. Employee training and development manuals.

12. Organizational charts.

13. Pre-meeting agendas and checklists.

14. Hiring checklist and packet.

15. Employee Training videos.

16. Pre-established disciplinary procedures.

17. Hiring process from ad to interview.

For a complete list of effective business systems go to www.the3dayentrepreneur.com/resources.

Centralization

The 3 Day Entrepreneur also knows that because there are so many moving parts in an organization, it can result in a massive amount of wasted time and effort in the day-to-day operation of the business.

Wasted Time = Wasted Money

Here are some interesting statistics on the cost of clutter and disorganization in terms of time and money in the typical business:

- The average American will spend one year searching through desk clutter looking for misplaced objects. *Margin, Dr. Richard Swenson*

- Workers lose 280 hours (7 weeks) per year by seeking clarification due to poor communication

- The average American spends one year of their life looking for lost or misplaced items at home and in the office. *US News and World Report*

- According to the American Demographic Society, Americans waste more than 9 million hours each day looking for lost and misplaced articles

- The Wall Street Journal reports that the average U.S. executive wastes six weeks per year retrieving misplaced information from messy desks and files. For an executive earning $75,000 a year, that translates to a loss of $9,221–12.3 percent of total earnings. For a company with one hundred executives at that salary, it translates to nearly $1 million in lost productivity.

- The average office has 19 copies of each document, spends $20 in labor to file each document, spends $120 in labor searching for each misfiled document, and loses one out of every 20 documents. They then spend 25 hours recreating each lost document. *PricewaterhouseCoopers*

- It costs about $25,000 to fill a four drawer filing cabinet and over $2,100 per year to maintain it. *Gartner Group, Coopers & Lybrand, Ernst & Young*

In order to combat waste, it is important to create a central database that can be easily accessed and provides up to date information for everyone in the business.

Centralizing Information

Centralizing information consists of creating a central location to keep all of the organization's systems, data, and documents, as well as keep them up to date if any changes are made. There is nothing that wastes more time than trying to find a piece of information when you need it most. It is even worse when you finally find the information, and later find that you used an outdated copy of what you needed.

This is why a central database of information has to have certain criteria to be most effective. These include:

1. **Accessibility**—It has to be located in a place where anyone in the organization can have access to it. This can be online, or at a central place in the office accessible by all who need the information.

2. **Syncing Ability**—Also, the database has to reflect all the up to date changes that have been made so that it can provide the most current and relevant information to whoever seeks it. It also keeps the previous copies in case someone needs to go back and research previous information.

3. **User-Friendly**—It has to be easy to use to find the information that is needed. Having an extensive database that is too complex to use is as much a time waster as not having one at all.

4. **Search Ability**—It has to have a function where documents or data can be easily retrieved by putting multiple types of information such as: the name, date, tag, or ID number of a document.

Best Centralized Information Systems

In the business world today, there is a great selection of information systems to choose from to centralize all of the information in your business. Here are just a few that are currently available:

1. **Remote Server or drop box with Syncing Ability**—Having a remote server that houses the company's entire database provides easy access, centralization, search ability and the ability to sync when-

ever new changes are made. It also brings a lot of security in case there is a concern of outsiders gaining access.

2. **Online Information System**—There are information systems that can be housed fully online, that can provide all of the needed aspects to centralizing information. The best part of this type of system is that it can be accessed anywhere in the world.

3. **Central Server**—Having a central server that is connected to all computers in the office or outside the office can provide the centralization necessary to stream line operations. User permissions can be given to people with different levels of responsibilities also.

4. **Project Management Software**—If you are consistently working on important projects, as well as storing information, there is software that can provide the capability to use both in a seamless process. It is user-friendly, and can provide additional services like To Do lists, assign projects and data to users, and provide notifications for deadlines.

Conclusion

You can create great leverage in the operations of a business through minimizing the amount of wasted time, effort, resources, and money used in the day-to-day operation of the business. This results from creating systems to keep the organization running efficiently and consistently. This also comes from creating a centralized information database to keep the organization on the same page in regards to the information that it manages.

PART V

The 3 Day Entrepreneur Challenge

Now that everything has been said, it's time to apply these principles in your life and business, so that you can reap the rewards that come from living the 3 Day Entrepreneur lifestyle.

Though we've spoken about hundreds of ideas and techniques in this book, you may be wondering where to start, in what order you should do everything, or what you should do now versus later.

Therefore, I have laid out a plan to get you living The 3 Day Entrepreneur lifestyle as soon as you can. Since we know that not all business owners have the same tolerance for risk, I have laid out three plans: a Super-Fast Track, a Fast Track, and a Conservative Track. Each plan is designed around a time frame that is within your comfort level for change, so that you will have the best chance for success.

The Super-Fast Track

For those that want to operate on the highest level starting today, we have created the Super-Fast Track. The Super-Fast Track is designed to help you create the greatest value possible, in the shortest period of time. In this track, we go straight for doing the 20% of tasks that bring 80% of the results; and only doing the 20%. This track is only for those that know in their heart of hearts that they were put on this earth to play big, and they will only play big, or not play at all.

Another requirement for this track is that you already have a source of income to take care of your personal needs. This is because the goal of this track is to create massive value first and foremost. It is designed to do this regardless of whether your personal needs are taken care of or not, so make sure you are set in this area.

Also in the Super-Fast Track, you will only deal with customers or sell products that can bring you revenues in the 5 or 6 figure range and above. Therefore, you should only participate if you are ready to operate with this level of customer and cash flow. The Super-Fast Track is only for the heart made of steel.

Expected time to begin seeing results: 30–90 days.

The Fast Track

For those that want to jump in feet first, we have designed a Fast Track process for helping you see great results in a short period of time. I must remind you that it is not for the faint of heart, but for those that have a higher risk tolerance than the conservative track, and who are highly driven by the capacity for success.

You will begin to see results within the first 3–6 months. This Fast Track is designed to be like buying a new pair of shoes, "the best way to break them in is to walk in them." The plan is laid out to throw you into a 3 day workweek and force you to do whatever it takes to make it work. Again, this is not for the faint of heart, but definitely for the adventurous and those seeking massive, yet quick results.

Expect time to see results: 3–6 months.

Conservative Track

For those of you that need to put your toe in the water and to crawl in a bit at a time, we have designed a Conservative Track that will ease you into the 3 Day Entrepreneur lifestyle. It is designed to give you a slow and steady system for getting yourself and your business to expand your comfort zone, and fit this way of operating.

You will see results, except they will come in small increments. However, those increments add up over time. Before you know it, you will be living The 3 Day Entrepreneur lifestyle and can enjoy all the benefits that come from it.

Expect Time to see results: 6–12 months.

So here we go...

CHAPTER
19

The 3 Day
Entrepreneur Blueprint

The 3 Day Entrepreneur Blueprint is designed to help propel an entrepreneur into producing the highest possible value in their business and life.

Let's start by reviewing some of the major goals you will be soon achieving.

Goals

The major goal of the 3 Day Entrepreneur Blueprint is to create the most value possible in the shortest period of time. The focus is on identifying the highest value tasks in your industry, and automating everything you can to create that value working 3 days a week or less.

Here are some of the major goals you will achieve by the end of this program:

1. **Begin working a 2–3 day schedule.**

2. **Identifying and begin ONLY doing the 20% of tasks that bring 80% of the returns in your industry.**

3. Identify you're A-level power team.

4. Identify your ideal customer and market only to the highest value prospects.

5. Establish the most valuable pricing strategy for your business.

6. Create the systems (Marketing, Sales, etc.) that will produce the greatest value for your organization.

7. Automate your operations for greater efficiency.

Now that you know some of your goals, we will now begin establishing the action steps that you need to take to begin living the 3 Day Entrepreneur lifestyle. However, let's begin by first setting up your new schedule.

The 3 Day Entrepreneur Schedule

As Parkinson's Law says, whatever time you set to complete a task, is the time it takes you to complete that task. By setting up your schedule, you will determine the boundary lines of your activities. Then it will be up to you to create your success within those boundaries.

Choose your new schedule according to your track (Super-Fast Track, Fast Track, or Conservative Track).

Super-Fast Track Schedule

1. Choose 2–3 days that you are going to get all of the highest value tasks done in your business, and eliminate all other workdays from your schedule. Remember you can also choose 4–5 half days as well, as long as you do not work more than 30 hours in the week.

2. Start your new 3 day schedule, either this week or next week.

3. Let everyone know you are closed for business on any other days but those 3 work days.

4. Do no work on your non-work days. Turn off your phone, and don't look at email the days you are not working. Set up a vacation email auto-responder to let people know you only answer emails on your work days. Put up the Do Not Disturb Sign.

Fast Track Schedule

1. Choose 3–4 days that you are going to get all of the highest value tasks done in your business, and eliminate all other workdays from your schedule. Remember you can also choose 5–6 half days as well, as long as you do not work more than 40 hours in the week.

2. (For slow starters) Begin working only 4 days a week the first 1–3 months, then 3 days a week the next 3–6 months.

3. Start your new 3–4 day schedule, either this week or next week.

4. Let everyone know you are closed for business on any other days but those 3 work days.

5. Do not work on your non-work days. Turn off your phone, and don't look at email the days you are not working. Set up a vacation email auto-responder to let people know you only answer emails on your work days. Put up the Do Not Disturb Sign.

Conservative Track Schedule

1. First 1–3 months: Every week eliminate 1 hour off each workweek.

2. Next 3–6 months: Choose 4 days you are going to get all of the highest value tasks done in your organization and eliminate all other work days from your schedule. Remember you can also choose 5–6 half days as well as long as you do not work more than 40 hours a week.

3. Next 6–9 months: Begin working only 3 days a week or 30 hours a week.

4. Let everyone know you are closed for business on any other days but those 3 work days.

5. Do no work on your non-work days. Turn off your phone, and don't look at email the days you are not working. Set up a vacation email auto-responder to let people know you only answer emails on your work days. Put up the Do Not Disturb Sign.

CHAPTER

20

The 3 Day Entrepreneur Action Plan

Now we can begin to apply your 3 Day Entrepreneur skills to your business to create massive value, while leveraging your time, effort, resources, and money.

Again, for each track, all of the following action steps should be done within the following time frames:

- **Super-Fast Track**—Do all the following action steps in the next 30–90 Days.

- **Fast Track**—Do all the following action steps in 3–6 months.

- **Conservative Track**—Do all the following action steps in 6–9 months

Leadership

Action Step 1: Task Management

1. Make a list of all the tasks that bring the greatest amount of value in your business. These are the 20% that brings the 80% of results.

   - Remember, value is determined by whether it brings revenue, profit, equity or all three.

- Identify the general and specific high value tasks that bring the highest value.

- Make a decision that these are the only tasks you will engage in ever!

For a list of all of the general high value tasks in a business go to www. the3dayentrepreneur.com/resources.

2. Make a list of all the things that you currently do that have no monetary return. (I.e.: running errands, filing, bookkeeping, payroll, etc.)

- Make a decision to eliminate doing all of these:

  - Super-Fast Track—Eliminate them in the next 30–90 Days.

  - Fast Track—Eliminate them in the next 3–6 months.

  - Conservative Track—Eliminate them in the next 6–9 months.

- Make a plan for how they will be done, or eliminated, since you are no longer going to be doing them.

- Remember you can delegate, defer, delete or outsource all of these low-value tasks.

For the thorough list of the low value tasks you should not be doing go to www.the3dayentrepreneur.com/resources.

Marketing

Action Step 2: Identifying Your Ideal Customer

1. Make a list of criteria that describe your ideal customer. Ideal customers must have the greatest long term value, are willing to pay your prices, and are the best to work with. Look at your current ideal customers and list their benefits.

2. Make a decision to do business with "ONLY" your ideal customer and no one else.

3. Make a list of current customers that are not your ideal customer. Attempt to either challenge them to be ideal customers, refer them out for a fee or FIRE THEM.

   • Super-Fast Track—Do it in the next 30–90 Days.

   • Fast Track—Do it in the next 3–6 months.

   • Conservative Track—Do it in the next 6–9 months.

Action Step 3: Identify Your Optimal Marketing Strategy

1. Make a list of all your successful competitors.

2. Research each one and identify their Optimal Marketing Strategies.

3. List the marketing tactics that always work in your industry, and which ones bring your industry the highest value customers in the market place.

4. Use this information to design a preliminary Optimal Marketing Strategy that you will test over the next 12 months.

To download the Ultimate Optimal Marketing Strategy Developer go to www.the3dayentrepreneur.com/resources.

Sales

Action Step 4: Design Your Optimal Sales Strategy

1. Design a process for qualifying (filtering) prospects so that you only do business with the highest value and ideal prospects.

2. Design a sales process that will create the most value for prospects, and will quickly and easily persuade them to purchase your products and services.

3. Establish a sales script that can successfully convert the most qualified prospects into sales, in one-on-one sales meetings.

4. Establish a presentation that can successfully convert the most qualified prospects into customers in a group sales meeting.

For a high value sales process that consistently converts leads to sales go to www.the3dayentrepreneur.com/resources.

Pricing

Action Step 5: Create Your Optimal Pricing Strategy

1. Make a list of the highest prices that you can charge for your products and services that will appeal to the highest value customers in the marketplace. Research the highest price points asked in your industry by successful competitors.

2. Choose a higher price point for your products and services and test them on your new customers.

3. Make a list of the best terms you can offer your customers for your products and services, which will provide the highest profit for the business, and convenience to our customers.

4. Design new terms for your pricing, and charge various fees for the use of unique pricing terms.

5. Test the new terms on your new customers.

For a list of different ways to create your Optimal Pricing Strategy, go to www.the3dayentrepreneur.com/resources.

Increasing Customer ROI

Action Step 6: Increase Your Customer ROI

1. Make a list of different ways to generate the most ROI per customer and highest long term value per customer in your industry.

2. Research your successful competitors to see how much ROI they are getting per customer and how they do it.

3. Pick the best strategy and implement it with your current customers.

For a list of different strategies to increase your ROI per customer go to www.the3dayentrepreneur.com/resources.

Finance

Action Step 7: Leveraging Finance

1. Make a list of ways to turn your current expenses into investments that can bring you a better ROI. Pick a few ideas and convert the expense into an investment.

2. List some spending guidelines that will help you spend in such a way that it creates an even greater ROI for the business. Only spend money if the expense meets all of your spending criteria.

3. Make a list of ways to put every dollar that you have saved to work, to make you even more money. Pick a few ideas and implement them right away.

For a complete list of ways you can leverage your finances go to www. the3dayentrepreneur.com/resources.

Operations

Action Step 8: Optimizing Operations

1. Make a list of different areas of your business and begin designing written systems for them. As you complete your systems, put them to work right away.

2. Make a list of different ideas to centralize all the information and communications in your business. Choose the best option and put it to work right away.

For a complete list of ways you can automate your operation go to www. the3dayentrepreneur.com/resources.

PART VI
Business Resources

Appendix A
Additional Business Resources

Here are some additional resources to help you take the next step to creating the financially free lifestyle that you are looking for.

The 3 Day Entrepreneur Video Training Program

If you are looking for a hands on program to help you begin living the 3 Day Entrepreneur lifestyle, sign up for our 3 Day Entrepreneur Startup Video Training Course.

It provides you with 30+ videos of step-by-step training to show you how to turn your current business into a 3 Day Entrepreneur business, or to show you how to create multiple streams of income working less than 3 days a week. You can find it at this link:

https://www.udemy.com/how-to-build-a-7-figure-business-working-3-days-a-week/

Sign up for this $499 course for only $49 by using the promotion code: PENAPROMO49.

Udemy Selling Success Training

If you would like a more detailed and step-by-step training on making money selling video courses on Udemy, then consider my Udemy video course titled: **"How to Make $1K–$5K Selling Video Courses on Udemy,"** which you can find at this link:

www.udemy.com/create-passive-income-successfully-selling-courses-on-udemy/

Sign up for this $499 course for only $49 by using the promotion code: PENAPROMO49.

Kindle EBook Selling Training

If you would like a more detailed and step-by-step training on making money selling eBooks on Kindle, then consider my Udemy video course titled: "Make $500–$5000 Passively Selling EBooks on Kindle," which you can find at this link:

https://www.udemy.com/make-passive-income-selling-kindle-ebooks.

Sign up for this $499 course for only $49 by using the promotion code: PENAPROMO49.

Amazon Selling System Training

If you would like a more detailed and step-by-step training on making money selling your own products on Amazon, then consider my Udemy video course titled: "**Make $1K–$10K Selling Your Own Products on Amazon,**" which you can find at this link:

https://www.udemy.com/how-to-make-an-extra-1k-10k-a-month-selling-on-amazon.

Sign up for this $499 course for only $49 by using the promotion code: PENAPROMO49.

Other Business Training Resources by William U. Peña, MBA

If you are interested in a full list of business-training courses by William U. Peña just visit:

https://www.udemy.com/u/willpena/

The 3 Day Entrepreneur Website

www.the3dayentrepreneur.com/resources

This website is a resource center of all of the best practices in business. You can access all of the references in this book, as well as more valuable tips and trainings that will help you start living the 3 Day Entrepreneur lifestyle right away.

References

1. The Illusions of Entrepreneurship—Scott Shane

2. Build a Business Not a Job—David Finkel

3. The Ultimate Sales Machine—Chet Holmes

4. The Challenger Sale—Matthew Dixon and Brent Adamson

5. Communication with the 4 Personality Types—Preston Ni

6. Organizing & Time Management Statistics—http://www.simply-productive.com/2012/03/time-management-statistics/

Other Books by
William U. Peña, MBA

Amazon Selling Secrets: How to Make $1K–$10K a Month Selling Your Own Products on Amazon

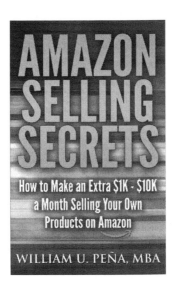

***Get Your Copy on Amazon Today!

Make an Extra $1K–$10K a Month in the Next 30–90 Days by
Passively Selling Your Own Products on Amazon

If you are looking for an additional passive income stream, there is no better way than to tap into the 74 Billion dollar marketplace created on Amazon.

By mastering the Amazon Selling System you'll learn about in this book, you will be able to easily tap into the opportunities on Amazon, and create an additional $1K–$10K a month in passive income.

This book will teach you the step-by-step system, and highly sought after secrets of how to identify highly popular products, and then transform them into your own special brand, which customers will pay a lot of money for.

Get Your Copy on Amazon Today!

Passive Income in 90 Days

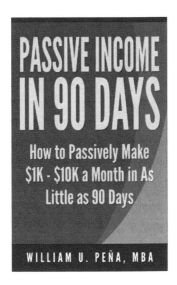

***Get Your Copy on Amazon Today!**

Learn 3 Simple Ways to Start Making $1K–$10K in Passive Income Per Month, in as Little as 90 Days

If you've ever wanted to know the secret to creating passive income in the quickest and easiest way—so that you can make extra money, or even replace your income...This book will give you the answers you need.

In this book, you will earn the secret to being successful at whatever passive income efforts you make.

You will learn about:

- How to use the Passive Income Success mindset to more guarantee that you will become financially free.

- How to use the Passive Income Success System to help you create passive income quicker and easier, and retire earlier than you think.

- Learn the many secrets of how to create passive income, even if you don't have a lot of money to start with.

- And much, much more...

So, if you're ready to get out of the "Rat Race," or if you're tired of trading time for money—and you want to create enough passive income to become financially free, then pick up a copy of this simple yet powerful book today—and learn how you can start doing it right away.

**Get Your Copy Today and Start Building
Passive Income Right Away!**

***Get Your Copy on Amazon Today!